Dedication:

For Wolf Moondance,

a visionary and shaman who has paid the price for her vast wealth of spiritual clarity and insight.

Aho,
Standing Wolf

A note from the editor

"A Visual Map"

With over 35 years in her field as an animal communicator, Samantha Khury has been featured on numerous television shows such as "Turning Point" with Diane Sawyer, various programs on the Discovery Channel, "Sightings", "P.M. Magazine", Regis Philbin's Morning Show", and "The Phil Donahue Show". Her documentary, "I Talk to Animals, A Portrait of Samantha Khury" has been shown on PBS, BBC, as well as other European stations.

I met Vicky Lee briefly in Brazil two years prior to a dinner conversation I had with her upon her return to the United States. This conversation changed the course of my life. I knew I was supposed to write about animal communication, but found it to be an arduous task that I had struggled with for ten years. Because of my frustration, I had been paying for help with my writing.

This is where that extraordinary dinner conversation comes in. Right in the middle of our dinner, Vicky put her fork down, looked straight into my eyes and said, "I know why you are not getting your book done. First of all, you're visually oriented. You need to see where you're going and what to do next. There are six books, Samantha, not one--- you're trying to put all that information into one book. You need a visual map showing the lay out and content of each book."

Her clarity regarding my ability to communicate with animals, my dyslexia and what I would be bringing to the public was awesome. She saw very clearly what I needed to do in order to accomplish my dream. That weekend we embarked on a psychic journey doing vision boards which mapped out each step. We created a vision board for three different stages of my life. We also drew charts that outlined the obstacles.

Her psychic skills bring with it tangible methods which helped me move the emotional blocks around my writing, as well as my personal growth regarding my marriage. I highly recommend and trust her spiritual clarity regarding each interval of my life and possible future prospects, which gives her an edge over a life coach.

As the editor of this vision board workbook, I helped Vicky to take her extremely honed psychic gifts and make them accessible to everyday people. Having worked with thousands of animals and pet owners on an individual basis, I understand how to cross the communication gap between species with compassion.

As her editor, I guided her to add an element of patience to her sharp-as-a-whip brain. Vicky works like a psychic surgeon. She sees, analyzes and organizes the "chaos" in your life in a split second, formulates an answer and then fixes it. Before you can process it, she's done and onto the next step. She's taken "self-help" to a more evolved level, developing it into a spiritual science. My role as editor was to help her explain what "psychic" is to a mainstrem audience who knows nothing of the paranormal and see how it can be applied on a daily basis to help people to discover their true soul map.

Love,
Samantha J. Khury

Samantha's vision board for inter-species communication

Vision Boards:

A Guidebook for Mapping Out Your Vision

By Olivia Vicky Lee

Painting on dedication page done by Samantha J. Khury

ISBN 13# 978-0-9788840-1-7
ISBN 10#   0-9788840-1-9
SAN # 851-8718
Body/Mind/Spirit
Bisac #OCC000000

© 2008 by

Taro Patch Small Press

Corporate Headquarters located in:

San Clemente, CA 92672

(949) 276-6427

visionboard@me.com

http://web.me.com/visionboard

http://visionboardworkbook.com

All rights reserved. No part of this book may be reproduced or transmitted in any form or by any means, electronic or mechanical, including photocopying, recording or by an information storage and retrieval system without written permission from the author, except for the inclusion of brief quotations in a review.

Table Of Contents

Chapter	Title	Page
Preface	I create psychic maps	2
Introduction	Your Vision Map	4
	How to Build Your Vision Board	12
Step 1	The Art of Learning How to Ask Questions	14
Step 2	What You Want: Changing Your Beliefs	16
Step 3	See Your Vision	24
Step 4	Create the Path	26
Step 5	Manifest Your Vision	29
	Lillian: Celebrity Philanthropist	36
1st Vision Session:	Calling in Your Spirit Guides	39
	Spirit Guides	45
2nd Vision Session:	Masks	47
3rd Vision Session:	Creating a Body Chart	62
4th Vision Session:	The Pyschic Core of Body Fat	74
5th Vision Session:	Who Am I Eating For?	88
6th Vision Session:	What does it look like when I eat only for me?	96
7th Vision Session:	Who am I feeling chubby for?	104
8th Vision Session:	When my best friend, "Fat," leaves me	114
9th Vision Session:	Money with Strings Attached: Revenge Fat	123
10th Vision Session:	Pyschic Attacks	129
11th Vision Session:	The Song of YES	146
Conclusion	Aloha	152
Acknowledgments	Mahalo Nui	153
	About the Author	154

Preface
"I create psychic maps"

In this book, I am going to take some rather sophisticated psychic and self-help tools and make them as user friendly to you as possible.

Although I use many standard tools such as meditation, prayer, chakra clearing, and feng shui, I mainly use my psychic abilities to communicate with your spirit guides, dead relatives, your higher self and "God." I map out your soul DNA, apply karmic "formulas" to old patterns, change core beliefs, look at past lives, retrain your brain to react differently in crisis, and identify the mythology underlying your life patterns and healing agreements.

What I do as a psychic business and life coach is work with corporate executives, small proprietors, sick and dying patients or anyone going through a major life transition and "map" out their higher life purpose in relation to their current situation and where they want to go.

If they have a particular goal in mind, such as making more money--- I ask them to simply think, meditate or talk about it.

I can literally see a map of their desire.

Meanwhile, a "psychic screen" quite like a blank movie screen appears in my mind. Within seconds, I can literally see a map of their desire.

It takes me another 10 to 30 minutes to explain what I see to my client. I see the shapes, colors, lines and graphs of their object of desire. I see paths leading towards it or out of it. I see other people's energies supporting them or holding them back. I also see obstacles, challenges and karmic patterns that my client continually re-creates which blocks him/ her from receiving what he/she wants. Then, I attempt to have my client build and draw this map from scratch in another 2 to 3 hour session.

Simply put, I help people to map a way to their dreams.

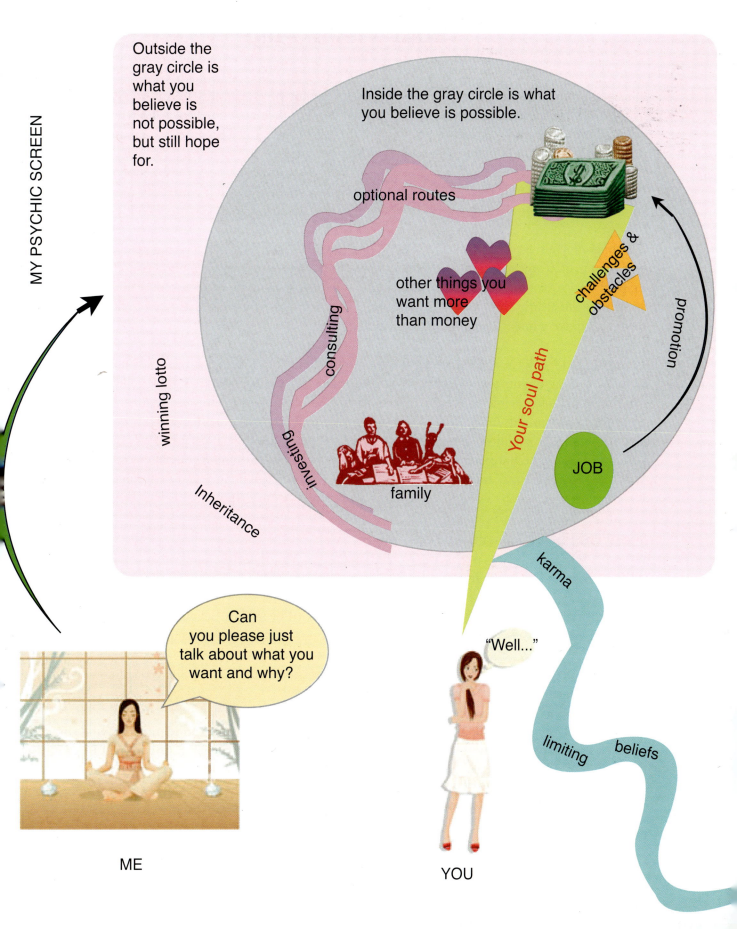

Introduction
"Your Vision Map"

This book represents the meat and bones of how I use my psychic ability to transform people's lives through therapy sessions. I've had clients tell me that they are "clueless" as to where to begin. I ask them simple questions about what their goals are, jot some notes on a paper and within an hour, we have an accurate map of their soul path.

I'm going to try to show you how I do this. Start with a sheet of scratch paper and a pen, jot some notes down and within several hours---- create an accurate map of your soul path.

The map of your vision of your life is as unique to you as your DNA. Everything you do from business/work/career to family/romance/home and adventure/passion/fun fits into the larger map of your soul path. It all works in harmony together. When one thing is out of alignment, your map will clearly show you how and why. That's why this is such a useful tool for anyone who desires to make a huge "leap" in their spiritual growth.

I am going to condense several weeks of coaching a client into succinct simple chapters with homework assignments and exercises. Please consider this a crash course. It took a lifetime for my clients to build karmic patterns which blocked them from living out their dreams. It has taken them profound insights and personal transformation to re-create new dreams. I am not going to stop to breathe or explain certain New Age or self-help terminology. I am going to assume that you are racing right alongside with me. Why? Because I want to change your life or someone you know in as little as 7 hours. I believe this book is a seed. You create the conditions in your life which make it grow into a magnificent tree, called your "vision map."

How this book is structured:

This introductory chapter gives you a snap-shot of how I work with a client.

In the next chapter, I explain how to create a vision board by asking, believing, seeing, creating and then, manifesting your vision. I devote one section to each of these 5 steps.

In the rest of the book, you will "sit in" on 11 of my sessions with Lillian. She is dealing with 3 core areas in her life: body, relationship and career/money.

Like many of my clients, she has built a model for how she lives her life, an identity for who she is and a karmic pattern with men. The first thing we do in a vision board session is what I call "anesthesia." Many times clients will not meet with me because they have either been molested, lost a loved one or been hurt deeply by an ex lover in their past. The older they get, the more innocent or tender that wound becomes and starts to show up in their lives through poverty, cancer or divorce. They feel that they will have to re-live or dredge up all that old hurt in order to excise or fully release its hold over them--- in order to become rich, healthy or in love, again. This is not true.

First Session: Anesthesia

When a client comes to me with a problem, I diagnose their "core wound" and explain it to them within the first hour. Then map out their entire lives in the next 3 hours. I show them how the patterns they have developed unconsciously and subconsciously have shown up over and over in their marriages, jobs and family life on 4 levels:

- Spiritual
- Beliefs / mental
- Emotional
- Physical

Usually, they are amazed that I can pinpoint directly how and when their patterns manifest the same reality over and over for them through a diversity of their personal experiences. Once they see that, they let go of all their resistances to this work because suddenly, all the craziness in their lives begin to make perfect sense.

For example, Cindy came to me on the brink of walking out of her marriage. She felt verbally abused and disrespected by her husband who had lost their fortune on a business venture and insisted on keeping the business open even though it continued to drain their finances. She felt like she had no choice but to leave him because it was useless trying to communicate with him.

We started by making a list of all her ex boyfriends. We made 2 columns: BEFORE and AFTER. We listed the characteristics of her boyfriends when they first began dating: romantic, financially well off, loving, athletic, treated her well, traveled together, fun, educated. Then, we listed their characteristics after she moved in with them or decided to commit to a long-term engagement: moody, lost job/income, stubborn, boring.

An "overview" map shows how your intentions have created everything in your life.

It shows your Higher Purpose in relation to those intentions.

And the actions, behaviors, attitudes and relationships that have resulted from your intentions.

On a separate piece of paper, we made another list for her current husband. It turns out that all her boyfriends were the same type of man: successful, fit, adventurous, well-rounded corporate executives. Cindy already knew that before we started our session. But then I pointed out that she was exactly the same as well---- an exceptionally pretty, high-income, athletic, fun attorney. She already knew that, as well. But then I drew a gray rectangle on our list in between the "before" and "after" columns. I asked her, "Would you agree that they are a mirror of you?" Being a lawyer who thinks in a practical and logical manner, she said, "Sure."

"It seems like they do a Jekyll and Hyde thing. Before you marry or commit to them, they are wonderful. After you move in with them, they turn rotten." I hypothesized.

"Yes!" she agreed that while her personality, physique and career-level stayed the same throughout time and commitment in the relationship, the men always changed.

"Let's look at this mirror," I pointed to the gray rectangle. "Every time you describe these men, it seems like you are talking about a PERFECT guy. He's the perfect mirror reflection of you."

"Yup," she responded. "That's why marriage always seemed like such a natural progression to the relationships."

"Your perfect picture," I drew an arrow leading the gray rectangle 'mirror' across the threshold of "before" and "after"---- "turns dark once you commit."

"Yes," she said.

"Your mirror is causing the men to turn from Jekyll to Hyde," I say. "Marriage is a huge deal to an executive who knows that once he commits to managing a project, he has to show success. Once he marries you, he better live up to that perfect picture of yours. If he fails, he knows you can always leave him for someone else. Look at you--- you are a perfect reflection of your perfect picture." Cindy is immaculate in her dress, health and speech. "So he tries so hard to fulfill that picture of yours, that he is willing to risk his life savings and your marriage in order to be a perfect picture of your perfect man."

Cindy has tears in her eyes. 3 of her past boyfriends went bankrupt in business deals after she moved in with them. So she knows that this is true. I continue, "They loved you so much, they risked all their money, fought tooth and nail with you to keep their businesses alive and lost their pride as businessmen because they didn't want to tarnish your perfect picture. They wanted to be the perfect man for you."

We looked back on the list we made for her current husband where we wrote down, "Did not follow his own spiritual path to be a holistic healer because the rewards were too small. Decided to imitate someone else's paved road and open up a large doctor's office, instead."

This whole time, Cindy felt like she was the victim in her relationships, suffering through each man's ambition to make it big and then losing all their finances as well as fighting day and night over it. After we made the "overview" map of her relationships, she realized that she had controlled the outcome of every single one of her boyfriends' and husband's behavior and career, from the start. These men had sacrificed themselves for the sake of her perfect picture.

Cindy concluded, "I'm the 'someone else' in my husband's list. He was trying to imitate my paved road instead of following his own path. That's why his business is not succeeding. He's not being true to himself."

I call this overview map of the client's entire relationship, career or body space, "anesthesia" because it releases their pain and resistance to exploring difficult or emotional issues. This usually takes about 3-4 hours.

I will book a second session with them the following week. By that time, they are willing to go into detail about anything because that was the hardest thing they've ever had to deal with it and it turned out to be not so bad. It also explained their entire history of relationships, body issues or money. It takes the mystery out of "why" things no longer work for them.

Second session: Diagnosis

Once we map out the client's karmic pattern in a specific area of her life, we begin to talk about goals or desires. I ask the client, "What would you like to achieve or have?" While she speaks about this, my goal is to try to find the client's "key questions." The answer to any problem is not important. Finding the right question is the key to unlocking the secret to everything that you have created in your life, good and bad.

I asked Cindy what kind of relationship would she like to have with her husband instead of the arguing which they are currently going through. She said that she wanted it to be like it was before they got married, when they were still dating. For me, this is re-creating the same relationship pattern all over again. When she said that, I heard her saying on a deeper level, "How can I turn Jekyll back into Hyde?"

If you ask the wrong question, you will get the wrong answer.

Learning how to ask the right questions, will guide you to the right answers.

To me, this was the wrong question. Even if I gave her a magic potion to slip into her husband's coffee and thereby gave her the perfect solution to her problem, the potion would eventually wear off, her husband would eventually develop a strong immunity to it and she would have to keep concocting new versions of the potion. This is a so-called "band-aide" therapy.

"Cindy," I said, "you have this tendency to walk out on all your relationships." She nodded her head. "When your perfect picture starts to deteriorate, there is no way to save it. It's just a photograph, a picture, a piece of paper, a marriage certificate. Let's make that picture real. Let's put it inside of you and create a true partnership, not just a picture that you can leave behind. Let's ask a different question."

"Okay," Cindy had a blank look on her face.

"Let's ask," I suggested, "what does true partnership look like?" I wrote down on her map, "commitment." Because she was so riveted by her husband as Hyde morphing himself into Jekyll and pre-planning her divorce settlement, I wrote down the key question I found in her map, "Where is Cindy?" Cindy took a crayon and scratched a palm tree into the corner of her map, a "one-way" sign and then drew herself escaping from the relationship on a jet plane.

I drew a black line above that map---- forcing it to be the bottom layer of our map. In that layer, I labeled it as a relationship between Jekyll and Hyde with Cindy running away. A trail of ripped up "pictures" followed her. I wrote in "His/Ours."

On the blank top half of the map I called it, "Both." I wrote in "His/Her." I told Cindy, "You've lost your identity to these men because they've lost their identity to your perfect picture. Where are you Cindy? In the top half of your map, we are going to draw you--- NOT as a reflection of your own perfect picture, but as you truly are in a relationship. You won't have to run away to go find yourself anymore. **You are going to have a NEW relationship with the SAME guy. That's the definition of commitment. NOT the same relationship with a new guy.**"

The answer is never as important as the question. Because the answer to every request is only what you believe you can receive.

If I ask for $500 but only believe I deserve $50. I will recieve $50. But if I ask. "How I can feel more deserving?" I can receive more than $500.

This is how asking the key questions can change how you map and envision the rest of your life.

Session 3: Treatment Options

I've classified the insights that my clients receive in our vision sessions into 3 categories:

1. smaller "aha" moments
2. breakthrough's
3. cracking the code

At any time, the client may be satisfied with their improvement upon a certain area of their life and then stop consulting with me. The "breakthrough" that Cindy had is that she went from thinking of herself as a victim in her marriage to the controller. And when we continued our sessions, my goal as a facilitator was to "crack the code" of her relationship space so that she could then create "commitment" and true partnership. I wanted to see her draw herself onto her vision board map as happy and present, rather than just running away or absent.

However, "cracking the code" of our key question, "Where is Cindy?" goes a bit deeper than just discovering how she re-creates the same perfect picture of her mate over and over again. It stems from childhood and growing up with an oppressive Japanese American father.
It involves finding a client's core beliefs--- both positive and negative. What are beliefs? It is something that society, your family, friends or others keep telling you is true or something that

you keep telling yourself is true---- until it literally becomes true in your reality. You imbue it with faith.

For Cindy, she believed that if she held up a "perfect picture" of her mate, he would be perfect forever. Her husband nearly bankrupted them in order to keep this picture from deteriorating. This is what happens. We would rather save our beliefs, keep them alive or in perfect shape----

> *I would characterize the smaller "aha" moments as me pointing out to a client the patterns that keep showing up in their lives. The "breakthrough" is when they discover exactly how they have created that over and over again. "Cracking the code" is when they harness the power of their beliefs that created that pattern in the first place---- in order to create something new.*

then change our beliefs and improve our situation.

I go through a list of exercises with my client in order to discover exactly what their core beliefs are. There are surficial beliefs we have that guide us on our daily route to school or work, such as "If I don't pay my bus fare, all the other passengers will know and hate me." Then there are more emotional beliefs like, "Men only want good women, so I can't let my husband know about my past." Finally, there are deep wounds or unconscious beliefs that run our entire lives. For example, "My father raped me when I was 5. I know that whatever I do, say, have or offer is inherently bad." Anything from relating to her husband to getting on the bus is driven from this core belief that causes my client to think of herself as "always being bad."

Once we find a core negative belief, we have to transform it into a core positive belief which is equal in power to the negative belief. We "flip" it over. An easy way to do this is to say, "I am always good," but the client may not sincerely feel that way. At times, we do more exercises to release grief or process the discovery of always feeling bad.

Or, we conclude that a positive belief that feels more true to my client might be, "Even at 5 years old, I knew that I had power over my father, sexually and emotionally. I compensated for this guilt through my relationships with men. Honestly, I felt sorry for my Dad. I wish that he, like all the other men in my life, were stronger and not weakened by the sexuality of an innocent kindergartener." It turns out, that the corollary positive belief of "I am bad" is "I have always been powerful."

A person might have 4 core beliefs that rule their entire lives. Another might have 18. It varies. If a client manages to change just a single one of their core belief, it has a huge impact on their life. I usually try to go for at least 3 core beliefs with each of my clients.

Session 4: Reconstructive Surgery

Thus far, we have created an "overview" map, diagnosed patterns that keep recreating the same reality and discovered core beliefs which cause us to insist that this reality is true or permanent. After constructing new positive beliefs to take the place of old negative beliefs, we are now in an ideal position to create a new "vision" of the client's life.

There are quite a few modes or modalities I employ in order to do this. First, we look at the old negative patterns. We look at its architecture and how it is structured. Then, we try to create something that leaves room for my client to get everything that he/she wants---- and not settle, make compromises, feel stuck or suffer for her choices.

Cindy had built her perfect picture to include a perfect mate (Dr. Hyde) and herself. Once she crossed the threshold of marriage, her mate turned into a "not" perfect husband (Dr. Jekyll) and she became absent from the relationship---- turning submissive, not speaking up for herself and trying to run away (divorce). This is an either/or pattern. Where we have either dating/good OR marriage/bad.

When we re-created Cindy's relationship map, we changed the either/or pattern to a model that included "BOTH" Cindy and her husband, Ben. I told her, "Ben is not Dr. Hyde. Ben is not Dr. Jekyll. Ben is Ben. Cindy is not Dr. Hyde's wife. Cindy is not Dr. Jekyll's victim. Cindy is Cindy."

Creating a new structure for a vision map involves changing from:

EITHER/OR to BOTH

WIN/LOSE to WIN/WIN

50/50 to 100/100

I labeled the new map "Cindy and Ben." In the old map, there was only room for Cindy and her perfect picture of her mates. The men did not truly exist as themselves in the old map. They were simply mirror reflections of her picture. Cindy for that matter, didn't truly exist in her old map. She was a "picture holder." The only time she really showed up in her old relationship map was when she was boarding a jet plane in order to escape. The old map was a series of torn pictures and broken mirrors. There weren't any real people. The new map has room for humans AND their relationships.

Another client of mine had created a 50/50 balance in her life as a corporate consultant who had a secret spiritual life at home where she meditated, did yoga and chanted. She came to me wanting to lose 50 pounds, have a spiritual epiphany and possibly a mystical experience with God which she called, "enlightenment." When we looked at her overview map which was split evenly in half between the corporate and spiritual sides of her life--- there was no opening to allow the energy of "enlightenment" into her life.

Her 50/50 model of her life kept her safe, but it also acted as a bubble to shelter her from any raw, true, intense or immediate "enlightenment" feelings or emotions. We started with a rectangle that was divided in half. Then, we went to a pyramid that was leading into a circular yin-yang symbol which better integrated her corporate with her spiritual side. But the tip of the pyramid had no divisions. It was a solid enlightenment zone where she completely did away with separating her life into compartments. She traded in her 50/50 corporate/spiritual model for a 100/100/100 prosperity/fun/enlightenment model.

Another client drew a map of her body which was a ruthless athletic machine, but there was no love or intimacy in either her map or her life. Her new map looked exactly the same, but where she had written "lust, purity, loneliness, power," she replaced it with "communion, friendship, balance." The physical layer of her map remained the same--- she will still be a beacon of health, but the spiritual layer of her map became more whole.

Overview Map

Each "overview" or starter map usually has 4 layers and 3 major sections. Here is an example:

	Past	Present	Future "NOW"
Spiritual			
Beliefs			
Emotional			
Physical			

The above map shows the 4 layers of your life (spiritual, beliefs, emotional, physical) as they go through time from past to future.

This is the autopsy of your vision board map. Everything is separated out so that we can analyze each of the sections in detail and make sure that there are no holes, gaps, missing pieces of information or energy. After we complete this map, everything should make perfect sense.

Meaning that when you look at your overview map, you are thinking, "Yes, this is exactly how I have designed my life thus far to get some of the things that I want and some of the things that I don't want. And in the 'future' column, those are the things that I believe I want."

The last step is combining all the sections into one grand-master map or what I like to call the vision board DNA, a snap-shot image of your soul as it travels timelessly through life within the eternal and powerful moment of NOW.

The 4 layers which seemed to have competed against one another will harmoniously intertwine to function as a single creative body called your soul DNA.

How to Build Your Vision Board
"A visual representation of your dreams"

A vision board is a large backdrop or canvas where you paste pictures of everything you hope to accomplish or have. It is a visual representation of your dreams.

The most conventional way of building a vision board is cutting out photos from magazines of cars, homes, the perfect body, living by the beach or other desireable goals and pasting them onto a posterboard. Other people write lists of what they want, such as the qualities of a future mate.

I believe you can manifest what you want by doing this. But "what you want" or what you initially think you want, won't necessarily give you what you need, are searching for or desire on a deeper, maybe even unconscious level. I believe that the **power of asking** must be learned with the same consciousness as one prays. Why? Because when you "ask," you are tapping into your highest creative potential. If you ask from a smaller place of fear or need, then you are not utilizing your full power. What you get as an answer to your request, will be a reflection of that smaller self within you.

As we age and our power grows, the journey becomes more significant than its destination.

For example, one might ask for a million dollars on their vision board. One might get it. But then, his/her family comes along and swindles them out of it. Or half of it goes to taxes and the other half goes to lawyers. The end result is practically the same as never having had the million dollars in the first place. Why? Because the energy utilized in asking for the money was from a place of lack. "I need this money because I lack something." And the universe responds by giving you the money, but does nothing to cure your sense of lack.

I combine traditional methods of Native Indian vision questing, New Age techniques of changing your beliefs and individualized processes when I help people build their vision boards.

==I believe that we are "creating," not "accomplishing" as we go through this life.== Many people try to force their visions to manifest into reality by making a vision board. I believe that the vision rises organically once you find out how you are going to integrate your higher purpose with your more mundane life. Finding out what truly makes you happy is a complicated challenge sometimes, as it keeps changing as you evolve through life. Also, as we age and claim more of our power and demand that our lives express this power--- our soul path begins to build a tapestry, not just a road leading from start to finish. Each step along the way grows more eternal and profound. The journey becomes more significant than its destination.

I want to make the whole process of self-discovery fun. Therefore, I want results NOW, in every moment. That means, I focus on the NOW journey, not the END journey.

PROCESS OF BUILDING A VISION BOARD

1. Asking questions

learning how to ask the right questions

answers are only reflections of how much you think you can receive or accept

Instigates desire

2. Believe

Truly believing that you can have what you ask for, involves a process of transforming your core beliefs from negative to positive

Finding out who you are

3. See it in your mind

you are inspired

you have a vision

your spirit guides are channeling insight into your brain

Understanding your life's purpose

4. Create the Vision

Mapping out the paths, roads and obstacles to achieve your goals

Taking action

5. Manifest your vision

without creating blocks

Learning how to receive

Step 1: The Art of Learning How to Ask Questions

Step 1: Get pointed in the right direction

The questions that we ask, point us towards certain answers. If you are in Chicago and ask how to get to San Francisco, you will be told to go west. If you ask how to get to New York, you will be told to go east.

Many times, a client will ask me a question. No matter how psychic I am or how accurate my answer is, if they are asking the wrong question--- we will point in the wrong direction.

So, I try to get them to "discover" what it is that they really want an answer to. What is the energy behind their question? Do they really want money? Or do they just want to feel safe? Because no amount of money will make them feel safe. There is no point in telling someone how to make more money and still have them feel as fearful as ever. The best advice is showing them how they can feel safe with or without money--- because once they feel safe, they will make wise decisions to ensure their financial security.

A client of mine, Angel, had to stop working because her cancer was progressing. She wanted to know if her and her husband would be okay, financially. The stress of her job as a social worker had contributed to her ill health for over 10 years. She called it, "compassion fatigue" which a lot of care-givers experience toward the end of their careers.

> *What is the energy behind the question you are asking?*

In my opinion, her worry over money was one of the root causes of her cancer. Although married to a successful engineer, she wanted to alleviate the burden of mortgage payments and their upscale lifestyle by continuing to work. She not only had compassion for her patients, but also for her husband. She loved him, dearly.

I believed that the universe had retired her by giving her this cancer and forced her to start asking different questions. Instead of, "Will we be okay?" I wanted Angel to ask her husband to ask himself, "Will I be okay, if my wife remains sick? How will I make the mortgage payments, so that Angel can relax and heal? How can I further support her in her happiness, right now?"

Step 2: Use your heart as a G.P.S. to direct you to your answers

The question that Angel was asking was pointing her in the direction of worrying (about money). The new questions that she allowed her husband to ask himself, helped her to focus on her own happiness and well-being. In a sense, she freed herself from thinking of her husband as another burden on her conscious. She also allowed him the space to become the sole provider and "step up" to being the man that he wanted to be.

His own soul path was wrapped up in her questions. When she expressed concern for him, I saw that he was miserable in his current position. He felt limited by his career. Her illness was forcing him to seek a more fulfilling and ambitious business route--- and it would give him the motivation and confidence to earn big bucks. When she stopped "mothering" him, giving herself the luxury of being weak for once in her life, she indirectly uplifted him in status. Both of them could move from "worry" to being taken care of, financially.

The "bottom line" or core of every question is this:

On a soul level, "What makes me happy?" or "How can I be happy?"
On a belief level, "How can I learn how to accept or receive more?"
On an emotional level, "Do I love myself?"
On a physical level, "How can I release fear?"

If you start by asking these 4 questions, you will be pointed in the right direction on your soul path. Sometimes it helps to ask yourself the same question over and over again, each time getting an answer which is more profound.

Step 3: Is your question big enough to receive a "big" answer?

How do you ask the right question? Well, what kind of answer are you willing to accept?

If you BELIEVE that you can only earn $1000 a week, the universe will accommodate the maximum amount of money that you are willing to accept and give you that. But if you change your belief and am willing to accept $10,000 a week, the universe is going to stretch to your maximum request. Your answer depends on your question. If you ask for $100, you get it. If you ask for $10,000, you get it.

But if you don't believe in the truth of your question, the universe reacts to your question like it was a pretend question or a lie and doesn't respond. The universe only responds to YOUR truth. And your truth changes based on your beliefs.

==The goal of asking a question is not to receive an answer. It is to figure out if your question is an accurate reflection of your desire AND your belief if that desire can truly be fulfilled by the universe.== When we ask questions, we are actually looking deep inside of ourselves and asking, "What do I really want?" and "What do I really believe that I can have?"

> *When someone asks me as a pyschic to give them the winning lotto numbers, I wonder if they really want to win it.*
>
> *Because no amount of money is going to make them feel rich if they believe that they have to win the lotto, just to create abundance.*
>
> *Why don't they give themselves some better odds at happiness?*

Step 2: What You Want:
Changing your Beliefs

We can use the overview map to chart out your entire soul path. Or we can use it to focus specifically on one area of your life, such as your career.

When you are just starting out and trying to make your own vision board, I suggest using the overview map as a basis. Pick one area of your life. In this section, I am going to use this overview map to focus on the subject of money.

As you will notice with your own vision board process, whenever you pick one area--- it acts like a mirror or a microcosm of your whole soul path. I used this map to help a client, Angel, talk about the pain in her body. We quickly found out, that her worry over money was tied into how she developed cancer.

In fact, when we look at the underlying architecture of how you think about money, sex, power, food, your body, relationships and your entire worldview, including how you see yourself--- we will find the "core" beliefs that rule your existence. The "laws" of your brain that govern your behavior and create all of your experiences, good and bad.

I call this the soul DNA. Other New Age teachers call it "core beliefs" or "core wounds." Religious leaders call them tenets of faith. Psychologists say, the shadow side. Freud called it the anima and animus. Jung labelled it as the collective unconscious. Novelists see it as mythology. Joseph Campbell called it the hero journey.

Below is the "archetype" of the overview map.

Level	Past (identity)	Present (life path)	Future (soul path)
Spiritual	karma	abundance	universal
Belief (Mental)	parents	value	social
Emotional	romance	experience	relational
Physical	ego	survival	personal
core positive and negative beliefs	(fixed) obstacles	(transformative) lessons	(open) opportunities

We start out in life as a lump of coal. We inherit our karma, parents, ego and are almost given or rarely choose our first intimate sexual encounter. Then, that rock or coal gets transformed through our life experiences into a diamond. As we age, we realize that it is not a diamond--- but a lens through which we view our lives. It key is not to change the rock or the diamond--- the key is to CREATE new points of viewing.

The Ego

The ego is a conglomeration of ideas about about WHO, WHAT, HOW, WHERE and WHEN we should be or act--- in order to survive in this world.

We are not born with these ideas. They are projected onto us by external "cultures" such as society, school, our parents and our relationships.

What we think we want, usually comes from these ideas. But what we truly want, comes from our being. We have 4 beings:

A spiritual being which is called the soul.
An intelletual being which is called the brain.
An emotional being which is called the heart.
A physical being which is called the body.

The world sends us ideas about what it thinks we SHOULD want. Those ideas stick to our ego membrane. Our egos are not solid and fixed. Think of them like lungs. They filter ideas from the outside world. We only breathe in or digest what we need from those ideas. Once we do that, our being "accepts" parts of those ideas that we like and forms its identity or "self."

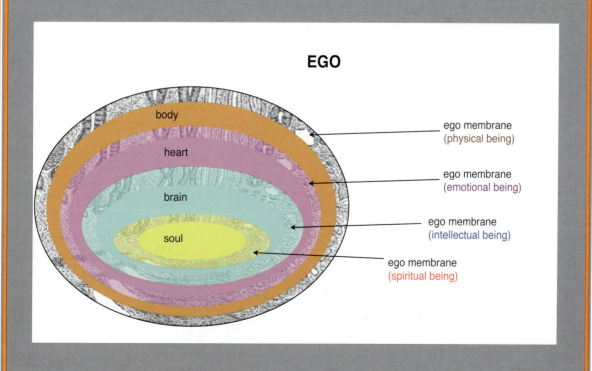

How you get what you want

This is the basic formula of how you create:

1. desire something
2. believe that you can have it
3. see the vision of it
4. be inspired to act OR wait to receive it
5. allow it to come into your life without blocking it

In this chapter, I am going to focus on steps 1 & 2. Most of my clients THINK they want money or success. They do. But they tend to want love or self-acceptance MORE than money, so they tend to manifest karma or life challenges which teach them about love or self-worth. They tend not to manifest opportunities that will give them money.

As their coach, you can see my predicament. If someone tells you they want money, but in reality they want love--- how are you going to help them if they aren't being honest with themselves? So I have to first get my client to realize or admit WHAT THEY TRULY WANT, in the order of their priorities. I do this by "charting" out what they say that they want.

"What you want" falls into 1 of 4 categories:

1. Spiritual: what your soul is choosing to evolve.
2. Belief: what you believe you are capable of achieving or having.
3. Emotional: what you desire.
4. Physical: survival and comfort.

A client of mine, Lillian, started to talk about money. I asked her what money meant to her. As she was talking, I made a list. She said, "travel, it means security for my husband and I, it means that I feel loved when I am able to take care of myself..." Every time she said something, I would write it down on 1 of the 4 levels: spiritual, belief, emotional or physical. So, I began categorizing what money meant to her, on each of the 4 levels.

It turns out that money wasn't piles of green slips of paper to Lillian. It carried the weight of a lot of emotions and pain. On each of the 4 levels, I separated the "meanings" of money into 2 more categories: positive and negative. Money also meant joy and love to Lillian when she was able to relax and "trust" money. Do you see how I was dissecting very quickly, everything that money meant to Lillian? After 3 minutes, I had a chart with a bunch of scribbles on it.

What does "what you want" mean to you on each of the 4 levels:

1. Spiritual: money means abundance.
2. Belief: money means how much I think I am worth.
3. Emotional: money means experience.
4. Physical: money means survival.

On a spiritual level, Lillian had a global vision of using money to empower those who dream of self-sufficiency. However, her karma was such that she had never been self-sufficient herself. In learning how to build her own business, she was learning that abundance sources from her faith in herself. Money was only a side effect of this realization.

On a belief level, Lillian's money set-point was at $10,000. This is the amount of money she was comfortable having. No matter how much she earned or spent, she always ended up with assets totalling no more and no less than $10,000. She wanted to change her money set-point to $1 million, but she believed that she was only worth $10,000. She got this belief from her parents and society telling her that women can't earn above a certain level of income.

On an emotional level, money gave her opportunities to experience life, travel, visit exotic places, exploring and above all, self-discovery. Money was a vehicle she used to discover more of who she was.

On a physical level, money gave her freedom to not depend on others. It helped her to become her own person, by letting her have her own car, home and job.

Money was not little green slips of paper to Lillian. If it was, she could just run out and earn some of those slips. The fact that she had so many blocks to receiving money and felt that she had to compromise herself to get it--- caused her to not like "money." She wanted it, but she didn't like it. If money were a guy, Lillian wouldn't date him.

On the positive end, money was a vehicle through which she could potentially have: abundance, self-worth, life experience and being her own person. In truth, she could use anything as a vehicle to get those things. She didn't have to project these goals onto money.

But how she uses or sees money---- is going to show us how she does and sees EVERYTHING in her life. It is going to give us a snap-shot of her worldview. Lillian's story is continued later on in the book. You are going to "sit in" on 11 of Lillian's sessions with me. But for now, I want to talk about Angel---- because she is a living example of how all 4 levels of converge.

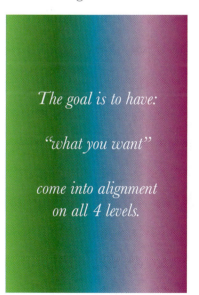

The goal is to have:

"what you want"

come into alignment on all 4 levels.

How does "what you want" show up in your life?

Angel had cancer. She wanted to know if this was "planned" on her birth chart. If her spirit decided before she was born, that from age 35 to age 50, she was going to experience lymphoma. Was this her destiny? Was this all pre-planned by her soul and God?

"No," I said. "You never plan a disaster."

"Then, is this a punishment? Did I do something wrong?" she asked.

We looked at the chart she did for her health. It said:

1. Spiritual: soul is searching for its purpose
2. Belief: my identity is as a sick person.
3. Emotional: I want to be make money and not be a burden.
4. Physical: cancer.

What you want on the spiritual level ALWAYS dominates. Your ego can fight your soul, but usually the ego loses as we age. I've known wealthy men who married beautiful young girls who stayed beautiful and young-looking throughout their lives. But the men still cheated. They could neither control nor understand their desire to seek intimacy outside their marraiges. For me, it was clear. Their bodies wanted the youthful wives. But their souls still longed for a real connection with a woman without fear or judgment, which is the what the ego provides.

Knowing this, I told Angel, "Your soul said that age 35, it wanted to start searching for its purpose. YOUR SOUL DOES NOT CARE HOW YOU CHOOSE TO LEARN THIS LESSON. If you decide to do this by ending world hunger or baking cupcakes--- it does not have any LESS or any GREATER value to your soul. Your soul doesn't care how your karma is fulfilled. It doesn't care how you choose to manifest learning your lesson. As long as you are fulfilling your soul's intention of searching for your purpose--- you are living out your soul path."

"So, I chose cancer to fulfill my soul's intention of searching for its purpose?" she asked. I nodded my head. "Why didn't I choose being a millionaire?"

"Because even if you were a millioniare and not a cancer patient, it would still FEEL the same. You would still be searching for meaning and suffering from denying your own power. The millions of dollars would feel like cancer to you. And your cancer, right now----" I pointed to her body, "is your million dollars."

Process of coming into alignment

"$1 million would feel like cancer?" Angel asked. "If that's true, then my cancer would feel like a million dollars."

"Yes, I can prove it to you," I replied. In the plethora of illnesses that Angel has had in the past 10-12 years, I asked her to choose just one.

She said, "Okay, how about B-cell lymphoma in 2005?"

"Great," I said. "Let's start there. Please tell me what that is."

She said, "It carries your lymph throughout your system. And lymph is fluid. Fluid is kind of like emotions."

"So if lymph is fluid and fluid is emotions," I said, "then your lymph is carrying emotions throughout your body. In other words, this cancer is a message-delivery system. It carries emotional messages."

Angel's cancer was a form of "carrying and communicating emotional messages throughout the body."

Somewhere in Angel's life, she stopped listening to the messages her body was sending her. Angel said that all her life, she tried to be invisible so that people wouldn't dump on her. When she was diagnosed with cancer, her body revolted. It wanted to be EXTRA visible by creating pain that Angel could no longer ignore or avoid. She was forced to care for her body almost 24 hours a day and dedicated the past several years to giving her body, her full attention. So the overall cause of her illnesses was "not paying attention" to her body's emotional needs, even the need for joy.

"Okay, now let's look at the cure or the benefit of having B-cell lymphoma," I asked Angel. "What else is this disease about?"

She answered, "Well, the doctors say that it's a blood disease."

I asked, "What does blood mean to you?"

She said, "What comes to mind, is blood nourishes my whole body. It keeps me alive. It is good. It is also rich."

"Okay," I said. "We now know the cause of this cancer--- which is not receiving the emotional messages that your body is sending you. We also know that if you acknowledge when in your life you did not listen to your own emotional needs, then you will receive the boon, benefit or gift of this cancer which is 'nourishing your whole body, keeping you alive, good and rich.' Basically, how you just described blood."

My theory here is that within each core wound is the power to heal that wound. Within each curse is born an inherent gift. Within each poison, lies the cure. So inside of Angel's cancer, there is both a positive and negative vibration AT THE SAME TIME. There is both a cause of disease and a cure for its healing. We wanted to find that secret, so I goaded her with a series of questions that I knew would lead to an answer.

The next question I asked was, "Was there another time in your life when did you NOT listen to your own emotional needs?"

She answered, "Well, when I was working at my job--- I hated it because everyone would ask me to nurse them or hold all their negative energy for them. But I didn't quit because I told myself that I had to pay my bills," she said.

When Angel was working, she wasn't jumping for joy every time she got a paycheck. She wasn't working FOR money because she loved money. She was working AGAINST the fear of not being able to survive. Money was a hateful source of stress for her. I asked Angel how she thought of money at that time. She remarked, "A life sentence. Toiling."

"How do you describe this cancer?" I asked her.

"Pretty much the same," she said.

"Because it is," I said. "For years, you denied the depression you felt on your job just to make a paycheck. You also blocked the thought of money, because it felt to you like a life sentence. Meanwhile, fluid is backing up in your body causing this lymphoma."

Money = blocked emotional messages
lymphoma = money
cancer = too much money backed up in Angel's veins

"You have MONEY CANCER," I said. "You have manifested money as cancer in your blood. The cure is to listen to the emotional messages that your body is sending to you. But since you haven't listened to your messages for 10 to 12 years, they're all backed up. You have so many messages coming to you all at once, that it feels painful whenever you listen to a few of them. You can't listen to your messages fast enough. They all want to be released from your veins. But in order for them to be released, they have to be listened to--- first."

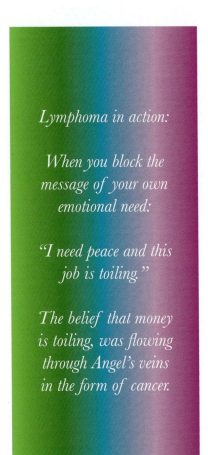

Lymphoma in action:

When you block the message of your own emotional need:

"I need peace and this job is toiling."

The belief that money is toiling, was flowing through Angel's veins in the form of cancer.

The Money Cancer Cure

In order to cure her cancer, Angel had to stop blocking the emotional messages of MONEY.

In her own words, money was telling her that it was good, rich, nourishing and keeps her whole body alive.

MONEY wanted to be her friend and co-creative partner. Money actually loved her, although for 20 years---- she had actively, consciously and purposefully HATED it.

"I'm so sorry, Money. You have been a faithful friend. I have abused you emotionally, just as I have abused the 'emotional message communication' system of my body (which resulted in cancer)," I suggested that Angel apologize to her own body.

Then, I suggested that she create a NEW belief around money:

"Money is a lover. Money is a friend. Money is a warm fuzzy. Money is power. Money is love. Money is fun. Money as it currently exists in my veins is a fountain of nourishing rich life."

Literally, Angel's veins became the corridors to her bank vault (which is her heart). They carried her belief about money to and from the heart, just like they once carried lymphoma.

In order for Angel to CASH IN on her $1 million sitting in her heart, she had to transfer the money from the vault THROUGH her veins into the palms of her hands where that lymphoma blood would magically turn into green wads of paper cash. How would she CREATE the transfer?

How could Angel apply this new money belief in her real life?

- yoga
- Latin dancing
- petting her kitty cats
- making love
- walking on the beach
- making her own healthy nutritious organic fresh juice.

Now, every time she felt PAIN in her body during yoga class, she had to think of another wad of cash getting stuck in one of her bank corridors or her veins. She had to coax it forward, "Come on money, you can do it. Just flow. Flow, baby. Mommy's right here, patiently waiting. I love you. I know you've been waited in my vault for 20 years to come out and so I will wait 2 weeks for you to subside. But sweetie pie, if you can come out within 20 minutes---- Mommy will be so happy!"

What would be the result of this new money belief/creation in Angel's life?

- Money would transform from "evil necessity" to loving friend.
- Angel was going to be really skinny, as the weight of all that MONEY weighing her down inside her veins was going to poop out of her veins and into her palms in the form of gold coins.
- Her bank vault (which was her body) would no longer be a storage area for old money, but a channel and a corridor for NEW life.

When Angel went back to yoga class and felt pain, she told herself,

"Let the money flow! It's coming out of my veins!!!"

All pain was the money fountain in ACTION.

Since Angel already manifested money as cancer, she was VERY close to manifesting MONEY as nourishing life-force that was good and rich.

Then, we looked at her chart that she drew in her first vision session. Where did she put money in her chart? In the emotional layer. Yes!!!! When we double-checked our work, it was accurate.

Money was the emotional message that Angel was blocking since 2005. She had to stop blocking the emotional messages and stop blocking MONEY. She had to become a money fountain.

Step 3: See It

I would like to recap the past 2 steps. First, we learned how to ask the right questions. This showed us what we really want or believe we can have. It also showed us that the vibration of the question must be an exact match to the vibration of the answer we expect to receive.

Secondly, we learned that what we want exists on 4 levels. All 4 levels must come into alignment for us to manifest what we want. The way that we do that is by discovering what our true beliefs are and then changing them to match what we want. In the case of Angel, she already had what she wanted--- money, only it was in the form of cancer inside her veins and not gold coins in her purse. So, sometimes the curse is the boon and the gift is the liability. She manifested the dark side of her power (which was her money cancer) and then flipped it over to see its light side.

This is the third step: seeing your vision. Thus far, we have only been trying to figure out if we are on the right path. No sense in building a vision board for the wrong path, right? But once we know that our questions, answers and beliefs are all matched up--- now we can ask for divine guidance.

We can do this through prayer, asking our spirit guides to show us the vision of what we truly want, or we can look back at our work and be willing to see it from a new perspective. We must be open to change. Changing what we want allows our souls to grow.

The Gift of (in)Sight

After doing steps 1 & 2, we come to realize that what we want looks a lot different than what we thought it looked like. For example, Cindy thought that she wanted Mr. Hyde and not Dr. Jeckyll. In reality, they were the same man. What she really wanted was neither Hyde nor Jeckyll, but a man who could relate to her from both his dark and light sides.

We have to see the truth of what we want, before we start building the path to get there.

DESIRE is everything.

What you truly want will always be a reflection of who you truly are.

Cindy's had to see that her path was "commitment." Her aim was for a relationship based on true partnership. Before, she thought that her path was "freedom" and her aim was to "trade in" her current husband for an upgraded version.

Lillian thought that all she wanted was income and came to me thinking that we were going to build a vision board based wealth. Instead, she had to see her business as a ministry which was based on love.

The truth was that money wasn't "cash" to her. It was about personal growth and life experience. She was unwilling to compromise helping her customers--- in order to "bait and hook" them with traditional sales techniques. She wanted to be wealthy in a way that fed and contributed to her global vision of "sharing," more than she wanted a lot of cash in her bank account. Thus, we ended up naming her soul path after her identity as a celebrity/philanthropist.

4. USE

When we use those messages, the blocks turn into "beliefs" that show us the intricacies of how and why we behave in certain patterns that keep giving us the same unwanted results.

5. OPEN

When we open up to changing those patterns, we create opportunities to have what we want.

OPPORTUNITIES

BELIEFS

MESSAGES

3. LISTEN

When we listen to those teachings, the blocks turn into "messages" that give us further insight.

LESSONS

2. CONTEMPLATE

When we contemplate them, those same blocks turn into lessons that teach us.

KEY QUESTIONS
KARMA
PATTERNS OF BEHAVIOR
CORE NEGATIVE BELIEFS

BLOCKS

1. LOOK
At first, obstacles look like blocks that stop us.

Step 4: Create the Path

Once we see the vision, it's time to create:

- new pathways to get us there
- people who will support us
- strategies to deal with blocks or inhibiting beliefs
- mantras or prayers that remind of us of what we are learning
- tools to empower us
- a spiritual dream team of spirit guides for both protection and guidance

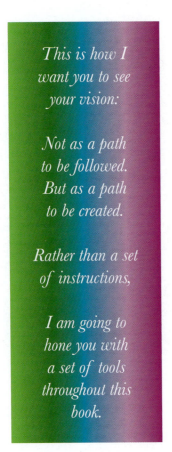

This is how I want you to see your vision:

Not as a path to be followed. But as a path to be created.

Rather than a set of instructions, I am going to hone you with a set of tools throughout this book.

Building Blocks:

Since I am a coach, I like to do things in a linear fashion. I like to show you what step A will look like, then tell you what step B feels like, then give you an idea of how step C might unfold. We are going to continue along the alphabet until we get to step Z.

Step A might represent poverty. Step B might be making sales calls. Step C might be developing confidence. Steps D, E, F, etc. are all steps which will lead to step Z. Step Z is earning a million dollars.

However, instead of watching you perform each step in succession---- we are going to be slightly more creative. Each of your steps are actually blocks or obstacles that keep you from success. They are your karmic patterns, negative beliefs and key questions. We are going to use these "blocks" to build your soul path.

Meaning, instead of saying, "Step B is making sales calls. I am going to make sales calls." We are going to use your "block" as to why you hate making calls to create another set of circumstances for step B to arise, naturally. Maybe you will go to a party instead and do all your networking in person.

We are going to do the same with step C, step D and so forth. When you realize that you can "create" each step spontaneously without having to follow any prescribed rules, you will start to skip steps. Meaning, the energy of getting over being afraid to talk to others is what you had to overcome. You didn't have to make sales calls.

When you realize how to work the energy underlying each step, you realize that you can eliminate the actual steps themselves. That's when you start skipping steps and start working "energy." Pretty soon, you learn how to create any kind of energy you want--- including making the million dollars without having to do any of the preliminary steps in between.

The Path

How are you going to employ those building blocks to create a life path that fulfills you or gets you to your goals?

We are not going to "draw" a path to your goals. We are going to use the building blocks to create opportunities to experience our own path.

How was Cindy going to create an opportunity for her to experience "commitment?" Going out and getting a divorce or a marriage counselor wasn't going to put Cindy on her soul path. But opening the door to allow her relationship to blossom into something called "commitment" or "true partnership" was.

She had to "walk the talk" regardless of the outcome, in order to both fulfill her karma and the longing she harbored within herself for deep intimate connection.

Old Way: Pre-determined Path	New Way: Creating the Path
We achieve by doing.	We create by being.
We "get" by action.	We experience by receiving.
We succeed by finishing a path.	We are happy creating a path.

How was Lillian going to create an opportunity for her to experience being a budding celebrity/philanthropist? By setting up her business as a ministry that helped people to merge their soul paths with financial success. Even though she was not a celebrity/philanthropist YET, she could give herself the feeling of being one and the chance to act like one to her current customer base. She could embody all that wanted herself to be, here and NOW, without having to wait until she finished climbing the ladder of success in her company.

For Angel, she thought that her path was crystal-clear---- how to get rid of cancer and heal herself. But actually, it was using the cancer as a teacher. What was her cancer teaching her about her own soul path? To get rid of the cancer was the same as getting rid of wisdom.

In addition to exploring the meaning of suffering and how it teaches us to appreciate and live in the present moment--- Angel found out that she was a global healer. Meaning, that she came down to earth to bear some of the karmic burden for a larger group of souls--- similar to what Jesus or Mohammed did. Her path was to reach nirvana, not to survive cancer. Cancer was her tool, not her enemy.

MANIFESTING

Here is a hint about how I work with clients. When you want something, in order to create it--- you either have to believe you can have it or you have to want it so bad that it hurts or makes you feel bad to not have it.

If you don't believe you can have it, then I have to push you in one direction or the other. I have to either convince you of the JOY of having it or exaggerate the MISERY of not having it. You can't create if you do not have a:

- strong desire
- or a belief that you can have it.

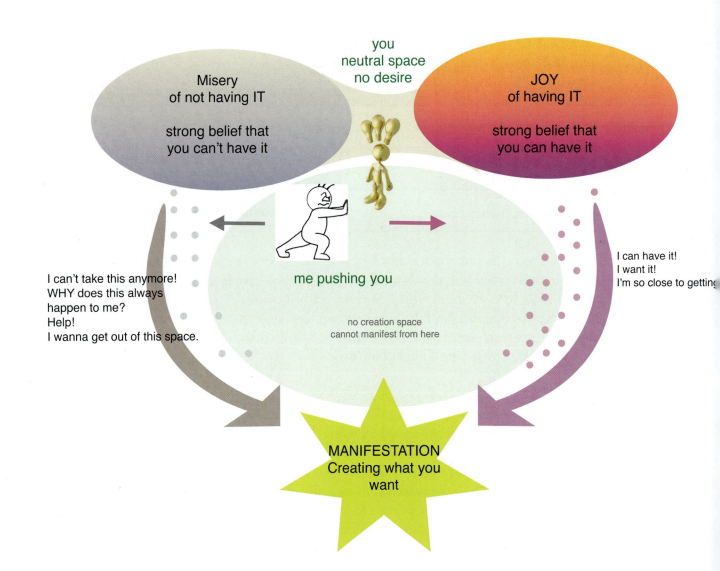

Step 5: Manifest the Vision
Without Blocking It

Seeing what you want from a truthful point of view should help you to shift your focus from wanting to have something more--- to being someone more. From achieving or finishing a path---- to experiencing, enjoying and learning while on your path. From judging your end results to realizing that your power lies in being able to create from the moment.

The next step is to allow your path to unfold, without blocking it.

Step 1: List your goals

We do this by drawing a picture of your vision, which shows what you want, the paths to get there, the people who will support you and the markers of success along the way.

For Lillian, a salesperson at a multi-level marketing firm, her goals were to go from "pounding the pavement in her high heels" to speeding down the highway of success in a Mercedes c-class sedan.

She also wanted to build teams of downline beneath her as a distributor. Eventually, instead of selling the product that her company manufactured, she wanted to sell herself and her success story--- in order to become a celebrity/philanthropist.

What you should have a vision of is:

the opportunity you are giving yourself to BE and EXPERIENCE your dream.

(not having or achieving it)

Step 2: List your obstacles

We also take the "karmic challenges" or lessons that you need to learn along your path and figure out strategies of how you will overcome them. For example, Lillian and I made a chart of her current status as a Lapis in her company. We called it "The Adventure Out" of Lapis Land and it featured a long highway that represented her path towards becoming a Ruby Duby, the next level of promotion.

We marked on her chart every challenge that she was going to face in Lapis Land. I asked her to list them. She started by saying, "my upline doubting my abilities."

"Okay, if this road to success is a highway--- then, would that be like a speed bump or something much more difficult to overcome, like maybe a construction zone?" I asked.

"It's more like a construction zone," she said, "because I can work on it, although it's going to take a lot of remodeling work. I shrink when the people above me, doubt me."

"What else is a challenge to you becoming a success?" I asked.

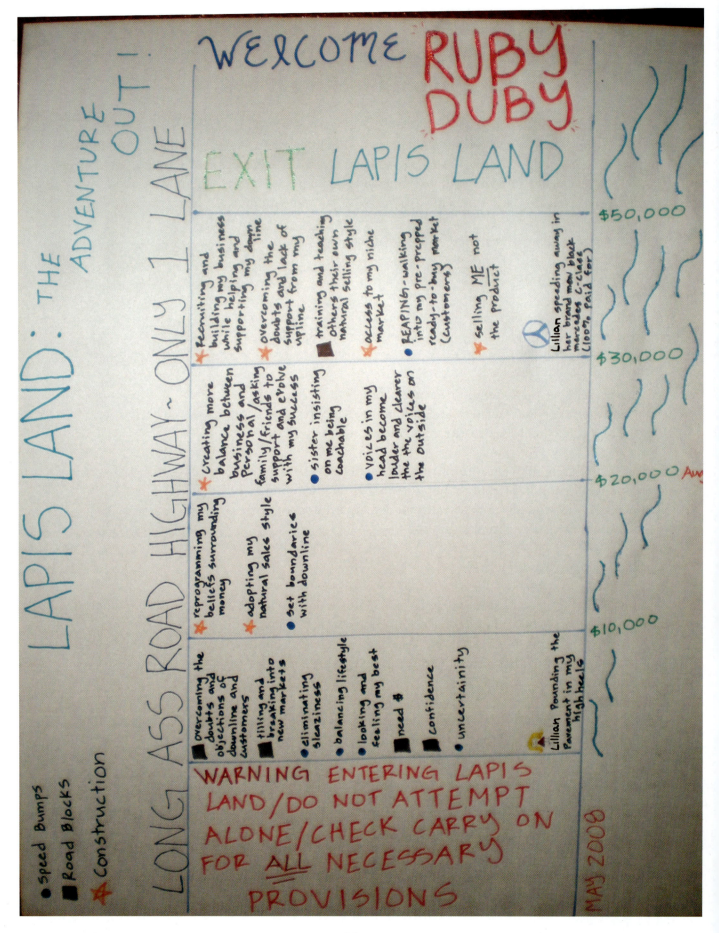

"Customers not calling me back," she said.

"Is that a major thing?" I asked.

"No. It's minor, I can get over that," she said.

"So, it slows you down--- but it doesn't inhibit you. You can get over that," I said. She nodded. "What else?"

"Oh gosh, probably trying to break into a new market," she sighed.

"If the road to success is a highway, then what kind of obstacle does that represent?" I repeated my question to her, trying to get her to formulate metaphors for all the challenges in her life.

"It's a road block! It stops me in my tracks," she answered.

"It seems like we've got 3 kinds of obstacles in Lapis Land. We have speed bumps which slow you down, construction zones which you need to work on or rebuild in order to move forward and then we have road blocks which completely halt you," I said. Lillian made map symbols next to each of her obstacles, to keep them categorized.

We also measured this highway in increments of monthly sales. When she earned $10,000 of sales, she faced challenges which proved to herself that she was capable. As she neared $50,000 in sales, she faced challenges which proved to others that she was capable.

We put the money in a flowing river next to the highway. The river got deeper and moved faster as she neared her goal. Small obstacles were like rocks that would sink to the bottom of her river and never even be noticed--- by the time she got to Ruby Duby. But at the beginning of Lapis Land, they were irritating even in shallow water.

Every time we looked at how she was going to overcome an obstacle, we did not think, "How is Lillian going to act? What is she going to do?" We thought to ourselves, "WHO is Lillian going to choose to be in this situation? How is she going to create something new from this particular set of raw materials?"

Step 3: Label the degree of "challenge" each obstacle presents

We continued to label each obstacle as either a speed bumps, construction or road block.

The next obstacle for Lillian was that a customer had purchased a few thousand dollars worth of products and returned half. She didn't know how to deal with the disappointment. "It's definitely a speed bump," she said. "I can get over this and move on."

"Great," I said. "What is the next obstacle?"

Lillian said, "There's going to be some big-wigs at this conference I'm going to. I don't have the confidence to banter with them like my sister because I feel like I haven't earned the right to talk eye-to-eye with them."

"So, confidence is the obstacle," I suggested. "Is that a speed bump?"

"It's a road block," she answered.

"It's that big?" I asked.

"It's huge. Without confidence, I can't even get up in the morning."

"Okay, what's the next obstacle?" I asked.

"I call some of my contacts to invite them to a presentation or a demo and they haven't called me back," she said.

"What kind of obstacle is that?" I asked.

"It's construction. It's definitely something I can work on, but it's going to take some time."

She thought about what construction meant, "When I think about construction, it's hopeful because the road will be in better condition after the work is done. If I call back some of my contacts with a sense of importance in my tone of voice, it would be better than calling them back with the same dejected tone, I usually use."

It really helped to talk about her obstacles in terms of building a smooth path to success or using the metaphor of the highway. She would recouch situations that normally made her feel helpless and incapable--- into constructive terms whenever I rephrased my questions.

For example, I asked her, "What do you see at road blocks? A lot of flashing orange cones, a detour sign, sometimes you see concrete blocks that keep cars from passing along the road. If your sister belittles you, does that really force you to take another route in order to get towards your destination?"

Instead of feeling defeat or a blow to her self-esteem, Lillian began seeing obstacles as just another road block to get past. It became a game to her with rules which she made up, herself.

Step 4: How are you going to deal with obstacles?

Lillian and I took each obstacle one by one. The first one was her customer returning half of the products that she bought. It was labeled as a speed bump. I asked her, "How are you going to deal with this speed bump?"

"I was cordial, of course, and gave her all the instructions on how to return products. But I still felt disappointment," Lillian answered.

"So are you just going to move over this speed bump?"

"Yeah, I'm going to skate past it," she said.

"That's one option. Let's think of other options," I said. She was drawing a blank. So, I offered, "What if your customer, Madeline, just loved the product---"

"She did!" Lillian interrupted me. "She loved it, that's why I was so disillusioned when she returned half."

"But what if she really loved it and…" I put my finger up to pause Lillian's train of thoughts, "and wanted to share it with all her friends."

"That's what she was going to do!" Lillian interjected.

"So she decided to over-buy products to make sure she had enough---- JUST IN CASE she ended up selling all of it. What would you rather have? Someone who buys $5,000 worth of products and returns half? Or someone who is worried that there is a slow or arduous return policy and decides only to buy $500? You see, you can give your customers this sense of SAFETY by allowing them to over-buy products by the thousands of dollars. Who knows? They might sell all of it. But you are helping them to think bigger when there is no risk."

"Hm," Lillian thought about it.

"Instead of glossing over speed bumps and pretending that they don't bother you, you could turn all your speed bumps into CUSHIONS," I suggested. "Think of the consequences of putting a bunch of cushions into Lapis Land Highway instead of speed bumps."

"You know what I think? Madeline really was only interested in buying 2 beauty kits which was $500 and I convinced her to buy 20 kits. She was so charmed by me that she wanted to show her friends the kit. So actually, I did make a much bigger sale than I had anticipated and it probably was the quick return policy that made her have no fear to buy so much."

We took Lillian's Lapis Land Chart and she wrote, ==“When I hit a speed bump, it can be a cushion if I want it to be. It can be a security and a safety, rather than a warning. It can help my clients move faster, not impede their speed because the cushion gives them no risk. Without risk, they think bigger.”==

"What's the next obstacle?" I asked.

"Confidence," said Lillian. "It's a road block."

"Okay, how do you deal with road blocks?" I asked.

"I just stop in the middle of the road and cry," she answered.

"How long do you cry for?" I asked.

"Until someone comes along and helps me," she said. "Like my sister or another up-line."

"So, you wait for help," I summarized. "Now, whenever we hit a road block--- what does it do? It forces us to stop. It does not allow us to proceed. Why? Because there is danger ahead. What kind of danger does 'not having confidence' present?"

"Well, it's dangerous because if other people help me, I don't get any credit for any of my successes. Potentially, I could move up to Ruby Duby and not know what the hell I'm doing!" she answered.

"Okay, what else? What does stopping you force you to do?" I asked.

"It makes me re-strategize and change how I feel, what I feel and intend. Maybe the universe is stopping me because I am about to make a big mistake--- like walking into the Team Elite meeting slouching and feeling like I'm not good enough. That is not the impression I want to make."

"Great," I said. "If there is a detour sign on this road block, what does it say?"

"It says, don't move ahead with this attitude."

"Great," I point to her original Career Chart, the first one we made during our first vision session. "It says here that you are a leader and a teacher. Do leader/teachers stop at road blocks and cry?" I asked.

"No. They find a way for their followers to get past the road block," she answered.

"You told me that your sister expects you to act like her sheep. She asks you to valet park her car or run errands and you do them. The 'Sheep Lillian' sits at a road block and baa's for help like a little lamb. She just obeys and can't rely on herself to make important decisions." Lillian nodded her head (like a sheep). "Every time you act like a sheep and hit a road block, you stop and wait for help. Well, Lillian--- you are no longer a sheep. You are a shepherd. You are Leader/Teacher Lillian and you have your own flock of sheep now. Your sheep are your downline and customers. They are relying on you to teach and lead them."

"They are waiting for me," said Lillian. "I'm not supposed to be waiting for help. Others are waiting for me to help them."

"Yes!" I exclaimed. "You are not a waiter. You don't 'wait.' In fact, the opposite is true. The universe is waiting for YOU to step up to your appropriate role. You are not waiting for your contacts to call you back. They are waiting for Leader/Teacher Lillian to call them back. They don't want to talk to Sheep Lillian again."

"You know what?" Lillian noticed, "At every road block I stand there and wait for the universe or the other party to do something different, instead of me putting my energy into changing the situation."

"Yes, turn this road block into a road opportunity. You have to get your sheep past this obstacle of 'confidence.' How are you going to do that?" I asked.

"I am going to say, 'Come on, sheep!' Let's go!" she waved her hand.

I paused. "Sheep are short and fluffy, you know. They have short legs." Lillian looked confused. "They can't climb over road blocks! They're sheep. You as a shepherd with your long legs can climb and get scratches all over your feet, but sheep won't do that. They're fearful creatures. So you have to find a way for them which allows them to feel safe. Sheep can sense when the shepherd is trying to get them to climb over a road block when the shepherd," I pointed to her, "has not created an open path and a smooth way for them, yet."

"How am I going to do that?" she asked.

"BE Leader/Teacher Lillian. Lead and your sheep will follow," I said. "If you are a good leader, the sheep will naturally love you. If you are not a good leader, even if the sheep love you--- they won't trust you to lead them and they will eventually follow someone else. If you want to be loved, you need to be a good leader--- not a waiter."

"I have to inspire them with confidence," Lillian thought out-loud. "I have to be their leader and they won't be afraid anymore. I can lead them by being an example."

Along the highway to success:

Turn every speed bump into a speed CUSHION.

Turn every construction zone into a classroom to improve your technique.

Turn every road block into an OPPORTUNITY.

We grabbed her Lapis Land Chart and because we ran out of space to write, we took a post-it and wrote, "When I come to a road block, I am responsible for my sheep. My flock is waiting for me to move the road block. Wherever I go, they will follow." We also wrote an affirmation, "I am not naturally a sheep. I am a natural leader."

Then, we wrote in the karmic lesson embedded into this road block, "Lillian's pattern is seeing Lapis Land as a road full of speed bumps, road blocks, hardship and rallying a team for help. Lillian's new creation: seeing all challenges and obstacles as cushions and opportunities. Building teams of down line which she leads into Ruby Duby territory."

On her chart, we also made a list titled, "As the newly crowned shepherd of Lapis Land, Lillian is going to deal with road blocks in the following ways:" Then, we bullet-pointed all her new strategies of how she was going to act like a confident leader and a teacher, instead of a helpless sheep.

Lillian
"Celebrity/ Philanthropist"

**Distributor and salesperson for a multi-level skin-care company
25 years old, Caucasian, lovely, honey blonde, full of positive energy
and attitude towards life**

For the rest of the book, you are going to sit in on 11 vision sessions with me and Lillian.

First Phone Conversation: Dealing with Hell

Lillian called me when she was at an all-time low in both her life and work. She had recently quit her full-time job as a waitress which provided her a full and steady income to become a distributor for an international skin-care company.

On the phone, she said that she had "major anxiety" and "depression" day-to-day from her job. "This is the biggest challenge ever," she admitted. "I just don't know what I'm doing at work everyday. I sit there at my desk and I'm not busy. I don't know where to begin to start selling these products. I don't know who to call or what to say. I'm just totally frustrated. Every morning I wake up and groan. I dread going to work."

"Why did you decide to join or work for this company?" I asked her.

She responded, "I went to a presentation and I just knew deep down inside, that I'm supposed to be doing this. It's based on a matrix compensation plan and…"

"Is that like a multi-level?" I asked her.

"Yes. There was a promise of all this money and…" she paused, "but the reality is that the business is unpredictable and the rewards are spontaneous." Basically, Lillian had mixed feelings about her work. There was hope, but also depression and anxiety.

"Okay, I felt like I knew enough about the negative aspect of her job, so I moved on. "What is your goal in working with this company? What do you want to achieve at work?"

She said, "To build a support-team of 15 other distributors across and 6 levels down."

"Is that like recruiting salespeople to be your downline and you get a commission off of everything that they sell?" I asked. I kind of knew what a multi-level was, but I didn't know the details.

"Yes, exactly," she answered.

"Okay," I said, "the first question that comes to my mind is where is your niche? Or who is your target customer?" When I'm talking to someone and they are asking me for help, I can "tune in" or open my psychic communication channels. Sometimes I ask someone a question just because I hear it as an inner voice inside my head. In other words, I was "directed" or "guided" to ask Lillian about her target market.

"Um, well that's the real problem. It's such an open market. This company just introduced this product to the United States. Prior, it was in Europe. But basically... I just have to rely on my own resources," she said.

"Do you mean that you sell to people whom you know personally?" I asked.

"Kind of," she sort of diverted my question. "It is overwhelming. The market is too huge. I'm all alone trying to build this business myself."

> *Key questions form the major rungs of your soul DNA.*

At this point, I had been jotting notes. I wrote down 3 bullet points:

- Anxiety
- Goal: to build 15 across and 5 lower levels of downline
- Key Question: Where is my niche?

Key questions are those that psychically "light up," for me. They not only tell me how Lillian is going to make money in the immediate future, but they also point the way towards her higher life purpose. When we find a key question at any point during our phone conversations or vision session, I always take time to right it down and put it aside in a special place. Key questions form the major rungs of my client's soul DNA.

While Lillian talked, I listened to what her soul was telling me. What I heard and felt was that there were two things that Lillian wanted:

1. Support/ a community
2. Her soul path which was bringing an element of herself to an existing brand/company/product

When I told her this, she said, "The first one is definitely something I need right now. The second one is something I dream about." She sounded doubtful.

> *Lillian's current growth period is called, "hell."*

"Now, let me just look into your space," I took a breath and relaxed, focusing on the "energy" of Lillian's anxiety. "Your greatest challenge, Lillian, is that you don't know what you want." As I said that, I felt this "stuck" feeling in my belly and frustration. I had an urge to eat fast food or caffeine to jolt me out of my stagnancy.

I continued, "That's why you have purposely put yourself into a situation where you can see what you don't want--- to force yourself to have some sort of desire or make a statement about what you do want.

"Not knowing what you want is kind of a hell because you don't know what makes you happy. You think you know what makes you happy---- what other people tell you what makes you happy or what you think will make you happy or what you rationalize in your head will make you happy. But emotionally, you're not feeling that gut-wrenching joy.

"It's not sourcing from some place deep and true within you. You think you are doing something that makes you happy. You are sort of making up conditions. Oh, if I made more money or had more friends, then I think I'll be more happy. You think you'll be happy, but you're not quite sure. You don't really know."

"That sounds just like me," she quipped.

"Fabulous," I said. "I'm going to call this stage of your growth period, 'your current hell.' When I see you, we are going to map part of it out."

OVERVIEW MAP
CAREER

	What I want that is tangible:	Higher Business Goals:	Angels/ Spirit Guides:
PHYSICAL			
EMOTIONAL			
SPIRITUAL			

First Vision Session:
"Calling in Spirit Guides"

I had only met Liliian for 10 minutes at a BBQ where she told me briefly that she sold anti-aging products and was "really confused" about her career. I gave her my business card and she called me a few days later. The only thing I knew about her when she called me was her job and what she looked like.

But once I talk to someone with the intention of psychically looking into their space and reading their energy, I have a general sense of their soul path. Just like how a doctor can look at your EKG, x-rays and blood test results and tell you something about your biology---- I can feel your energy and tell you quite a bit about how you're doing on your soul path. But like the doctor, I know nothing of your personal life, your likes or dislikes, what flavor ice-cream you prefer or even your personality. Most of that is extraneous information in terms of what I do, because I don't need it in order to help you create an accurate and profound diagnosis and map of your soul.

The difference between me and a psychotherapist is that you don't have to bear your emotions, past abuse or even divulge intimate details of your relationships to me. I can ask a few significant questions and glean the specific information I need from you, without having you go into a diatribe about your life. Just like a cardiologist isn't interested in your whole diet history, food addictions or emotional attachments to what you eat--- he only needs to figure out how many grams of saturated fat you consumed in the past 2 weeks, in order to determine complications with your medication. Or he may want to know what percentage of carbohydrates you consumed were combined with fat in the past 2 years to analyze why your arteries are blocked. I'm also specific about the kind of information I ask you.

The first thing that Lillian and I did was an "overview" map of her career. We took a big sheet of newsprint paper (18 by 24 inches wide) and divided it into 3 columns: what she wanted immediately, longer term goals and identity. Then we made 3 rows: physical, emotional and spiritual.

I asked her to fill in the details and she did. After she did that, I told her that in her fantasy world--- we can cheat. We are going to pretend that she can have anyone in the Universe as her spirit guide. They are going to be her personal support team in the spirit world and give her advice whenever she feels in doubt at work.

"Who would you like to have as your spiritual advisors? You can pick anyone, even a made-up or fairytale figure," I said.

> *Set up an agreement or contract between you and your "dream team"*

"Yes," I said. "What kind of help do you need in order for you to achieve your goals? To make it to Team Elite, be groomed to become a celebrity philanthropist and have more confidence in yourself?"

After some discussion to what she areas she would like help in, we came up with this list. Lillian gave each of her spirit guides a name which she preferred to call them:

> *Your "dream team" of spirit guides must fulfill every one of your needs.*
>
> *Think of them as an entourage of personal assistants and highly evolved mentors, some with knowledge and expertise within a specific field.*

- **Aquarius**, the high priestess of Egypt. She is the grace and elegance coach of the universe. She acts as a consultant to royal families.
- **The Beauty Goddess** shares beauty secrets with me, directs me to find the perfect clothes for my shape and helps me look radiant.
- **The Business Matchmaker of the Universe** finds customers and puts them in front of me.
- **The Event Planner of the Universe** invites me to the best parties and networking events where I can make big sales. He's in charge of my schedule.
- **Donald Trump and Suze Orman** act as my financial advisors.
- **The spiritual entourage of Oprah Winfrey** who are going to groom me to become a celebrity/philanthropist.

During our first phone talk, Lillian confided in me that a lot of her customers would seem interested in her product at first, but later change their minds. I asked Lillian, "When Business Matchmaker puts people in front of you, they might not be completely ready to buy the products or join the company as your down-line. So can we be more specific about what kind of people you need Business Matchmaker to bring to you? What is the profile of your perfect customer?"

After Lillian made a long list of the qualities and characteristics of her perfect customer, I drew a yellow circle around the list and said, "That's your job. Business Matchmaker's job is to put quality contacts in front of you. Your job is to turn those quality contacts into your perfect customer."

I was creating a boundary between what the Universe was going to do and what Lillian was going to do--- forming an agreement between her and her "dream team" of spiritual advisors. If she agreed to take this path toward her goals which she outlined as: success, trusting in who I am and celebrity/philanthropist; then the Universe will agree to teach and advise her along the way.

Homework Assignment #1: Using Your Dream Team

"Let's look at your goals," I pointed to Lillian's chart. "In your physical layer, you wrote 'Team Elite.' Which one of your spiritual advisors is going to help you this week on that?"

"Business Matchmaker, for sure," Lillian tapped her marker on his name. "I want to be busy this week with people to call, meet and sell products to."

"Great," I said. "When you go to meet with them, do you just make the sale right then and there? Or is there more to it than that?"

"There's more to it," she answered. "I have to look good or else I don't feel confident."

"So which one of your spiritual advisors is going to help you look good?" I asked.

"Beauty Goddess," she answered.

"What meetings do you have planned this week to test out your dream team?" I asked.

"Ugh. I have this network marketing event on Thursday that I am dreading going to!"

"Why?" I asked.

"Because all these big-wigs are going to be there and I can't face them. I don't know what to say."

"Give me an example," I asked.

"Mark Greenberg. He's the V.P. in charge of product development. When I see him, he's going to ask how I'm doing with my events."

"How are you going to answer him?" I asked.

"I'm going to say that I don't really have anything going on right now."

"Okay, let's look at your chart. You wrote that you wanted to be more confident on your emotional layer. You aren't acting confident in front of Mark. When are you speaking with him this week, I want you to imagine Aquarius standing right behind your shoulder and giving you advice. When you

> *Your dream team is a temporary band of guardian angels, who don't heal or save you. But who teach and guide you.*

walk into that meeting, Beauty Goddess would have dressed you, Aquarius is going to make sure you stand with poise and elegance, Donald Trump and Suze Orman will be schooling you on how to close deals and the spiritual entourage of Oprah will be training you how to be a future celebrity/philanthropist. So, when you walk into the room, you've got an invisible dream team who is standing behind you. That's a lot of power. Your dream team will have put a lot of energy into grooming you, so you have to keep up your part of the agreement by getting what you want out of that meeting." I pointed to her chart where it said, "friendship, recognition, respect."

"Your homework assignment is to bring your dream team to work with you and listen to what they're telling you," I said. "One thing you mentioned to me on the phone was that you feel alone in this business and that the isolation is bringing you the greatest amount of stress. From now on, you are not alone. You've got a dream team tagging you wherever you go."

Results:

Lillian came back the next week, ecstatic. Usually, she has no one to call or meet with during the week. She sits in the office and feels sorry for herself. But this week, her phone was ringing so much that she had to turn it off at night to sleep. She almost felt like complaining that customers would call her at midnight or 2 am to ask questions about the products, but then she remembered that it was probably Business Matchmaker helping her out. Also, she received a bonus check in the mail from work for $500 that she was not expecting. She told me that when she went into her networking meeting, she was shining and made a lot of contacts with people she would not necessarily talk to.

"I just pretended that Aquarius was standing right next to me and we were working the room. I even felt a little bit aggressive," she wrinkled her nose. "Normally, I would hide in the corner until my sister or someone I felt comfortable enough with would come talk to me. But this time," she smiled, "me and Aquarius were looking for targets or people we wanted to talk to. I became in control!"

She continued, "At one point, I started to slouch when the V.P. came up to me. Then I said to myself, 'No! I want to talk to him. In fact, come here, Mark!' And then we had an awesome conversation."

"Did he ask you how your sales were?" I inquired.

"No, he didn't mention it," she recalled. Then her face got sad. "If he did though, it might have shattered my mood."

"What would Aquarius whisper into your ear, at that point? How would she be coaching you to answer his question?" I asked.

"She would just look him in the eye and tell him that I have no sales this week," she guessed.

"Or," I offered her another option, "she might have told him that she's got nothing so far, but a lot planned for the rest of the month. And it doesn't matter if she makes no sales for the next 2 months--- she's learning how to hone her skills. She's positive she's going to be a success in this business. She'll make some sales when she's ready. Then, I think Aquarius would smile and be gracious because she thinks of herself as one day, being bigger than the V.P. himself."

"Oh," said Lillian, "just turn it around completely."

> *Quick fix homework assignments change your approach to life from "difficult with painful consequences" to fun and experimental.*

"Something like that," I said. "Until you develop more genuine confidence in your sales skills, just use your dream team to fake it for now. Because you can't do any worse at your job than you are now. So let's use this buffer zone to practice with your dream team. Act like a successful millionaire even though you don't feel it yet. Just as an experiment."

By doing this, it may not have brought in major income to Lillian--- but it relieved her daily anxiety of getting up every morning and showing up to work. It also made a depressing job, fun. It no longer was about success and failure on a daily basis, but about experimenting every day with her dream team. It wasn't V.P.'s interrogating or judging her. It was about her using them as practice to learn how to apply her "poise and elegance" techniques in a public setting. Because Lillian was so down in the dumps, a homework assignment that totally flipped her approach to her job from arduous and frustrating to fun and experimental--- even empowering, worked like a quick fix. Now that I felt like Lillian had some tools to deal with anxiety, we could move on to examining her core beliefs.

Using Your Dream Team

Situation at Work:	How I would normally respond:	Which Spirit Guide is helping me in this particular scenario?	What this Spirit Guide advises me to do:
Mark, the V.P., sits on my desk, leans over and asks me, "So, babe, what do you have going on this week?"	I answer in an apologetic tone, "Well, I don't really have anything going on, right now, Mark."	Business Matchmaker	Look him in the eye, lower the octave of my voice and assert, "Absolutely nothing." Then, smile and put my hand on his shoulder. "Actually I have 2 key contacts scheduled for next week and it's going to take me every hour I have until then to prepare for it. If I make those sales, I won't have to work for the next 2 months. That's how important it is for me to be completely free of appointments this week."
Team Elite networking event	Wait in the corner for someone I know to come up and talk to me.	Aquarius	Stand up taller. Look into the crowd for someone you want to talk to. Go up to him/her, introduce yourself and be gracious. Make a connection which will mutually benefit the both of you.
The Executive Director is upset and crying about all of her problems before we start our presentation	Comfort her and try to come up with solutions for all <u>her</u> problems	Financial Advisors of Donald Trump	Tell her to check her problems at the door. You came in with great spirits and ready for this presentation so forget about her problems and go shine!-!!

Spirit Guides

We all have spirit guides.

The exception is if you are a "dark" soul such as a mass murderer or a psychopath. Dark souls have no guidance from the "Other Side" or what most people consider to be Heaven. They are "abandoned" on the Earth plane and chose to "fall from the light" in order to become a dark soul. They reincarnate over and over again without ever visiting the Other Side in between lifetimes. Thus, they do not learn.

Then, there are a variety of souls who are in between the extreme dark and the light. They are called, "gray souls." They have not chosen to live for "good" or "bad." They make up the majority of souls on the Earth plane. About 2/3 of humanity are gray. They have soul paths and are just like everyone else. But they do not manifest great challenges or lessons in this lifetime. They may just be hanging out or existing, seeking pleasures or whatever makes them feel comfortable. They do not seek to make leaps and bounds in terms of higher consciousness.

About 1/3 or less of humanity are "light" or "white" souls. These are the people who have chosen to live for the purposes of "light" or their own godhood. They often have a "mission" to either save or uplift another soul--- or to better humankind. They also want to evolve spiritually, emotionally or otherwise. They teach just by example. By merely existing and surviving, their lives become a testament to their own humanity.

Light and gray souls all have spirit guides. It is commonly believed among psychics that you have at least 1 or 2 guides who stay with you throughout the duration of your lifetime. They are similar to guardian angels in that they protect and watch over you. But they are uniquely "human" or trying to learn more about the human experience by acting as your guide.

Many of them have had lives on Earth before. Some of them haven't been "physical" for centuries. But all of them live on the "Other Side" or what we refer to as Heaven. Where they exist, it is pure positive love. With that "cheat sheet" of knowledge, they help us on our dark plane called Earth--- to evolve our souls during our lifetimes. They are there to assist us in our personal growth.

A spirit guide can also be an aspect of your own nature, guiding you. Usually, I call that your higher self. I believe that we can also call in "extra" spirit guides as helpers or temporary guides that come in for a short period of time to help with something specific, such as a bad marriage or cancer. I have seen clients who had as many as 15 spirit guides surrounding them, as they walked through my door for a vision session.

Whether or not you have a predetermined set of spirit guides or a revolving door of guides, you can always ask for more help. Whenever a child or anyone says a prayer in earnest, a beam of light shoots up from their heart into the heavens. Following a single thread inside a myriad of glowing spider web veins, angels are sent down to Earth to answer each prayer. The only reason we would not be able to receive conscious insight of their response is if we block the answer with our own doubt.

How to call in your spirit guides for assistance:

1.   Quiet your mind
You can either go to a lake or a place in nature where you have solitude from the plethora of "voices," distractions or stresses in your life. I would suggest going somewhere away from your family, coworkers and loved ones. Or, you can set up an area in your home that is comfortable such as a chair or a place outside on your patio.

2.   Utilize a sacred object
This can be a notebook or journal. It can also be a blanket that makes you feel "wrapped" or "held" by the spiritual forces which will come in to aide you and help you to focus. It can also be a candle or a fire pit. It can be the sky. It gives you something where you are going to project your thoughts onto when you get a moment of profound clarity and insight.

3.   Set your intention
What do you want? Ask a question. Tell God what you need an answer to. Just hold that in your mind for a second. Then, imagine that you are sending forth the energy of your question out into the sky or the universe as an "offering."

4.   Say a prayer
Close your eyes. Imagine that a white light is surrounding you. You can use other colors as well, such as pink for self-love, green for prosperity or growth, purple for higher consciousness or awareness, gold for god-centeredness, orange for balance. Feel what each color means or represents to you and use that.

5.   Communicate
Pour your heart out. Scream at the ocean. TALK to your guides. Share with them your dilemma. Talk to the universe like you are talking to a psychotherapist, a counselor or a best friend. It helps to say your most intimate secrets.

6.   Meditate which cleanses your mind
Be still. Resist the urge to walk away, get a coffee, smoke a cigarette, eat something or make a phone call. Your body is going to make excuses about WHY you need to leave, right now. It is going to get uncomfortable.

7. Listen
Notice your thoughts. Let them pass. Let each thought pass out of your mind. Wait…

In the midst of your pain, boredom or peacefulness--- you will begin to have a second "wave" of thoughts. Listen. Don't filter them. Just notice them. Soon, your own thoughts will start "talking" with you like you are having an imaginary conversation with SOMEONE--- but not you. This might be a spirit guide. It might be God. It might be your higher self. But this "someone" is going to give you some wonderful, funny or heart-rendering advice. Listen…

7.   Write it down
You've got to document communication from your spirit guides. Later on, re-read what you wrote. It will surprise you. Sometimes, your guides will tell you a piece of psychic information that you can confirm months from now. Or, the advice they gave you will have new meaning when you are more ready to understand it.

Second Session:
"Masks"

Masks are the personas, attitudes or "roles" that we play in our relationships. For example, a woman might take on the duties and concerns of a wife and mother to her husband. But while he is at work, she might be cheating on him and acting like a lover or mistress to another man. If the role that we are playing in a particular relationship does not encompass the totality of who we are--- then I call that a "mask."

It's similar to a theatrical role in a play. We take on new "roles" and we leave old roles behind us as we grow up. However, throughout life, we often keep old roles just for fun or for play. We take on the "mask" of a hot young coed when we get drunk at a bar, even though we are 40 years old. Or, we put on the "mask" of an obedient daughter when we visit our parents for Thanksgiving.

We use masks like make-up, to cover up or hide who we really are. We also use masks to pretend to others that we are other than or less than--- who we are. And those masks force others to see us through this lens or filter--- that the mask creates over our true identities. So, we can control how others treat us by putting on a mask. They respond and relate to your mask, instead of to you.

This is quite useful for specific purposes. For example, if a woman wanted to seduce her husband, she could put on the mask of "hot slut." For a night, they could both forget about the kids and household bills. But when our masks are not conscious to us, we can easily get stuck in a single role in life or feel limited by them---- because they do not allow us to relate to others through the totality of who we are.

Many women I know have various masks which they wear for different men. I'm positive that men wear masks, as well. For example, to interest a woman, a man might act more athletic or more like a jock than he really is. For another woman who is more taken with wealth than youth, he might emphasize his career successes.

When a client comes to me and tells me that they are unhappy and want a higher income, health and love--- what they are saying to me is that they currently are making less money, not as healthy as they would like to be and single. I do not look at

> *Masks are the personas, attittudes or "roles" that we play in our relationships.*
>
> *We live through our masks. They regulate our behavior towards certain individuals.*
>
> *When we wear our masks, others respond and relate to our masks, instead of our true selves.*

their current situation. I look at what they want--- and that is how I identify them. I thought of Lillian not as the unsure pretty girl she felt like in her present moment, but as the capable strong and wealthy businesswoman she told me she wanted to become.

Because of this, anything less than what Lillian's goals are---- I consider a mask. I call those masks, "small Lillians." The Big Lillian is the real Lillian to me, the one who has already achieved wealth, fame and success.

Recognizing Masks

While Lillian and I were reviewing how her week went, she told me about a meeting she had with a 30 year old millionaire who owned several businesses and said he wanted to sign up as one of her downline. However, when she got to the restaurant for the dinner meeting, she realized that he was only interested in her. It was a "date."

"Were you okay with that?" I asked.

"The old me would have been. I would have went with whatever the guy wanted and allowed it to be a date. But then I started hearing Business Matchmaker and the entourage of Oprah telling me to get what I want out of this meeting: a business contact." She paused. "So I threw my shoulders back and kept steering the conversation back to my products and how we were going to work together."

"How did he respond?" I asked.

"He kind of went with it, but then he ended up evading it. He kept trying to change the dinner from a business meeting to a romantic date. I felt like I was fighting him, not letting him drag me down to his level." Lillian seemed sensitive about this issue, she had tears in her eyes. "He wanted me to be the old Lillian who would shrink back and do what the man directs her to do, even if it was a change of plans. I wanted to be empowered Lillian who is seen as a capable businesswoman, not a little girl."

"So here, we found one of your masks. It's the old Lillian who is seen as a little girl. That's the role you have played a lot in your past relationships with men?" I asked. She nodded her head. "Let's try to find more of your masks. We are going to make a list of all the men whom you've ever dated. Then, we are going to list how each of them treated you. Were they responding and relating to the real Lillian, the Big Lillian? Or were they treating you like one of your masks, such as 'little girl Lillian'?"

> *To make a man chart, categorize or stereotype each significant male relationship in your past and current life. Include relatives, platonic or nonsexual ones as well as past boyfriends or lovers.*

The Man Chart

Step #1: Make a list of men

We started off by listing all of Lillian's past male relationships. I asked her to write down all the names of all the men she's ever dated. I drilled her on how long they hung out, what the men looked like, their jobs, ages, quirks, etc.. I kept asking her the questions faster and faster so that she had to think quickly and categorize the men into easily identifiable statistics.

Step #2: List their characteristics

For example, instead of telling me how her and Brandon met, what Brandon wanted in life, his favorite food and his grandmother's dog--- I cut her off and asked her the "jist" of their relationship.

"Well, we never kissed because I wasn't attracted to him," she got right to the point.

"But you liked him as a friend?" I asked.

She hesitated, "I liked the attention." I paused and thought about it while Lillian admitted, "I wasn't attracted to him, but he was attracted to me. I liked how he treated me and it was fun... for a while."

"Okay," I moved on. "Next guy."

Step #3: Put the men into categories

As Lillian kept listing more men, it turned out that she had a bunch of guy friends whom she hung out with for a short time--- who were attracted to her, but she was not attracted to them. I asked her why all the friendships didn't last, since they weren't technically dating. "Well," she laughed embarrassed, "When they found out that they weren't going to get anywhere with me, they left. I never heard from any of them again." She had to think about that one, but she was pretty sure that they were all gone.

Step #4: Color code each category of men

"Hm, can you please highlight all those names in blue?" I handed her a marker. "What are we going to call these guys--- the platonic ones?" I asked.

"The friend zone," said Lillian. She already knew a nickname for those dudes.

"Okay, let's go through the rest of the names on your list--- the ones that are not highlighted." I was planning on going through the names one by one, just like we were.

But Lillian was able to sum up the rest of the guys like this, "All these guys are boyfriends."

"Were you attracted to them?" I asked.

"Yes, it was mutual. But I didn't have as much freedom when I was with them. That's why I had to have my friend zone guys, so I could just relax and do whatever I wanted in front of a guy. The friend zone guys liked me no matter what. But with Don, my last boyfriend…" she sighed. "I had to look perfect, act just like he wanted me to in front of his friends, I couldn't eat too much…" she kept on talking while I blurred out the literal meaning of her words and tried to get a sense of the "energy" of the boyfriend guys.

"Were they all the same type of guy or different?" I asked.

"They were all alpha males," she said matter-of-fact.

"The what?" I asked.

"The alpha male," she said again, "the top dog or jock on campus, whom all the girls want to date. He's arrogant, the center of his universe, he always has friends who look up to him, he's accepted by society and favored. He's treated special because he is better than everyone else."

```
Jose        - fun
Aaron       - 2 months
Crazy Ashton
Ali         (loved him)
            brother was
            nice
Sam (CUTE!)
Jonathon
(got sick of him)
Jared       (ate a lot)
            together
Robin  (6 months)
Norris (grandma - sweet)
Sierra  (River Rafting
Don
```

"Oh," I paused. "Why did you want to go out with them?"

"Because of the status. I get to be the alpha female when I'm with them," she answered.

"Okay. Highlight all the alpha male names in pink," I handed her another marker. "So now we have two groups of men: blue and pink," I pointed to her page.

As a summary, the names highlighted in blue represented the "friend zone." The "friend zone" guys were the ones who were attracted to Lillian, but she wasn't attracted to them. She kept them around because she felt safe, supported and accepted for herself. In essence, they were like brothers who took care of her and hung out with her, but never pressured her for sex.

The names on Lillian's list highlighted in pink

represent the "alpha male" and all of Lillian's ex boyfriends. They were the B.M.O.C. or "big man on campus" types. The fraternity brother or most popular guy in high school who all the chicks wanted to date. He was usually the best looking, richest or strongest among his social peers.

Step #5: Finding Your Masks

"What were you like when you were with the friend zone guys?" I asked.

"What was I like?" she seemed confused.

"Yeah. We talked about how the men were. They knew that you were out of their league, but they still had hope. So they were always excited to hang out with you, flattered by you just showing up. But what were you like when you hung out with them? Were you a snob or you were extra nice because you felt sorry for them?" I gave her possible answers to my question.

"No, I felt great. I actually felt more like myself around the friend zone guys than I did around my boyfriend, Don, even though I wasn't being intimate with them. Because I could act, dress or do whatever I wanted to and they would still accept me. So it was great while it lasted."

"But there was no romance or sexual contact?" I asked.

"Right," she said.

"So, you weren't really their pseudo girlfriend. You were more like a buddy?" I suggested.

"More like a sister," she corrected me.

"And why did you go out with them if you weren't attracted to them?" I asked.

"I felt desired," Lillian said softly. "I could do whatever I wanted to, be whoever I wanted to be. They liked me no matter what. I never had to worry with them because I could come and go freely as I pleased. I got to be myself."

"In a way," I said, "you were using them to build your ego?"

"I'm sure I was," Lillian said.

I laughed, "They didn't care because they got to be with

Lillian's 2 major masks with men:

As a sister in the "friend zone" where she was safe, supported and more sexually powerful than men.

OR

as the girlfriend of "Alpha Male" whose sexuality dominated their relationship and he was the "star" of the package duo.

you, a very pretty girl who'd otherwise not go out with them. How did that make you feel?"

"I got to be the prize!" she announced, happily. "It was all about me."

"Okay, write that on your chart," I said.

==This was Lillian's first mask: sister.==

"What were you like when you were going out with Don?" I asked.

"One thing that bugged me about Don was that he would treat me differently if something I did or how I dressed or looked, didn't please him. I remember him wanting to show me off to his fraternity brothers. That was kind of cool, kind of flattering. But at the same time, I never knew if I was good enough for him."

"I think of him as sort of a control being," I said, "unpredictable."

"I didn't know what the rules were with him. I felt like he didn't communicate that with me, so that it would keep me guessing," she said.

"How did that make you feel? Let's write it on your chart," I suggested.

Lillian ended up scribbling that she felt like she had to suppress herself a lot and pretend, so that Don wouldn't blow up at her. She blew back at him and broke up with him numerous times, but always went back to him. "I was afraid of being abandoned and left alone," she said.

"So, besides not being alone--- what did you get out of it?" I asked.

"Well," she raised her eyebrows, "I got to be admired for being his side-kick. Once, we went to Vegas and I looked really good for him. I was wearing a short black dress and when we got out of the car he took my hand, looked at me and said, 'Baby, I don't want you to be bigger than me. I want to be the star.' And I cringed."

"How did that make you feel?" I asked and pointed to her chart for her to write it down.

She scribbled, "Angry. Wanting to get him jealous and make him see that I'm admired by other men."

"At the same time, you had this status, yes?" I asked.

"Yeah." She wrote more, "I got to be the chosen one who the most popular guy wanted to date."

==Lillian's second major mask she wears with men is "girlfriend" or "alpha female."==

"Lillian's Man Chart"

FRIEND ZONE	middle	ALPHA MALE
SISTER	column	GIRLFRIEND
brother safe and supported accepted for who I am	(leave blank for now)	boyfriend threatened/ controlled status of "I'm with him"
respect my boundaries I feel desired I am alone They are going to leave me when they figure out that they won't get any further, sexually. I am always waiting for them to leave. I can be myself, natural Freely come and go Easy It's all about me I am the prize Could be anything I want Using my seuxality to get what I want No games/ I am already worthy Tell my friends the victory story I use them Arm candy Fun / casual Mutual/ balance/ half half/ care-taking/ honest/ genuine Supporters Temporary, no risk I don't care what they think		I have to do what he likes Does not accept me for who I am I am not alone. I'm with him. Get what he wants, sexually I don't feel desired I am waiting for the opportunity to leave him I had to pretend and supporess a lot Guilt Uneasy Can't I just be me? I get to be admired for being his side-kick Protected I am the "chosen" one Status Expected to be the perfect mold Angry Holding back so much Never feeling good enough to be with him I want to prove to him that I deserve his attention and to be treated special Effort/ lots of work I really care what he thinks I tell my friends my victim story. I feel used He uses his "alpha" sexuality to manipulate me.

Step 6: Your true self without masks

From Lillian's chart, we saw that she was either the sister to a guy--- respected, treated well, accepted and slightly more powerful than him OR she acted like a girlfriend and gave up her power, acceptance and respect in order to share in his "alpha" status with him.

On her chart, we ended up titling the 2 columns of men "EITHER" sister / "OR" girlfriend.

"You're either these guys' sister or you are their girlfriend. But you are never friends who sleep together or intimate companions sharing mutual attraction. There is always a power imbalance. Either you are more powerful and have a stronger sexuality with the friend zone guys or the alpha male's sexuality dominates the relationship and makes you feel lesser," I said. "What would it look like if Lillian built a relationship with a man that was not either a sister OR a girlfriend---- but BOTH friend and lover?" I asked her.

We drew in the middle column of her chart and labeled it "BOTH."

"What would your ideal relationship be like?" I asked her.

Lillian wrote into her chart that she wanted to have a best friend who is also a lover. "Like a partner in life?" I asked her.

"Yes!" she said. "Someone whom I can grow with, learn with, have an emotional bond with..." she kept listing out characteristics that described the perfect combination of personal growth, business success and romantic passion. "I want to feel a sense of importance, like having a witness to my life. I want to feel like we are a team, a package deal, together. And we support each other's dreams."

In each of the "EITHER" and "OR" columns, Lillian had to sacrifice part of herself to be in relationship with these men. In this "BOTH" column, she wrote down her relationship to herself, "Being me all the time," and underlined it 3 times.

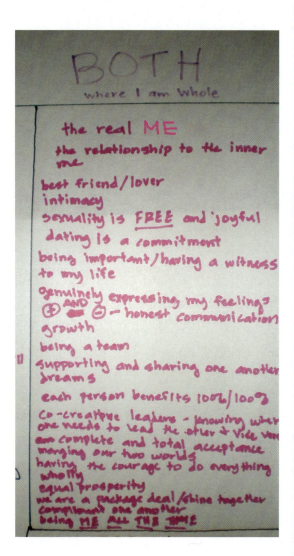

54

Step 7: Finding the "core" of your map

Lillian's 2 major masks were "Sister Lillian" in the "EITHER" column and "Girlfriend Lillian" in the "OR" column. In the "BOTH" column, she wasn't wearing any masks. She wasn't limiting or degrading her behavior or her identity in any way. So we chose to call her "the real Lillian" in that column.

"So all these men," I panned my hand over the 2 columns of men, "not a single one of them was spending time with the real Lillian?" I asked her.

She looked at her map. "No," she admitted.

"None?" I asked again.

"No," she shook her head. "Because even when I was being myself with the friend zone guys, I was just waiting for them to leave me. It was always temporary. As soon as they figured out that they weren't going to get any further with me, touch-wise, they took off."

"Did that hurt your feelings?" I asked.

"No. I expected it. I didn't care. There were always more friend zone guys."

"But only 1 alpha male?" I asked.

"Yes, just one of him and many of his admirers," she said.

"So in the EITHER column, there are a bunch of disposable men who admire you. And in the OR column, there are a bunch of women who want to be with the alpha male, but you are the one who is with him." I drew the equation for her.

"Yeah," she agreed.

"So the question still remains," I said. "When the real Lillian comes out--- who is she with?" Lillian was silent. "You've never dated a guy as the real you?" I suggested. She shook her head. "Okay, then tell me who dated these friend zone guys. Name some of your masks that you wore with them."

We listed it on her chart not only "Sister Lillian," but "Little Girl Lillian" who needs to be taken care of, "Arm Candy Lillian" who acted as the hot date of the friend zone guys, "Independent Lillian" for her carefree and easy persona when she was with them and "Victory Story Lillian" who could brag to her friends that she had this guy whipped.

Then, we listed the masks she wore when she was with her alpha male boyfriends. We wrote, "Girlfriend Lillian," "Prom Queen Lillian" who is envied by other women and who feels special, "Wife Lillian" who has to worry about her boyfriend's approval all the time, "Victim Story Lillian" who complains to her friends that she is sick of being in a relationship with her alpha male in order to get pity and attention, "Sorry Lillian" who never feels good enough and "Worker Lilllian" who has to prove to her alpha male that she is worth his attention.

Once we had all of Lillian's lesser masks, I wanted to combine them all into one major mask. I wanted to combine all the "sister" masks with all the "girlfriend" masks and give it a name.

On the bottom of Lillian's chart, we wrote "Intention." I asked her, "What was your intention in going out with the friend zone guys. You told me what you got out of it in detail. But sum it all up for me. What was the ONE thing, the underlying motivation of going out with these guys?"

"I wanted to feel loved," she said. We wrote it down on her chart under the "friend zone" column.

"How about going out with Alpha Male?" I asked.

"I wanted to feel important, like I matter," she said. We wrote that down on her chart.

"The real Lillian already loves herself. The real Lillian already knows that she is important. So who was it that was not feeling loved? What part of you didn't feel important already in her life?" I asked her.

She kept looking at me, trying to answer my questions. I repeated them, "Who... or when in your life did you not feel loved?"

She had tears in her eyes because she got what I was insinuating. That ==this chart is not about her relationships with men. It is about her relationship with herself. The men don't treat her like her mask. They are mirroring to her, how one small part of herself is treating the rest of her.== The real Lillian bifurcated herself in order to have relationships with men. She split herself into being either the empowered sister to these guys or being their submissive girlfriend. But she never got to be both with one man.

"Who or when in your life did you not feel loved?" I asked again.

"I just keep thinking of my mom," Lillian was crying. "When I was 7 years old, she took me to the doctor to ask him why I was so chubby. I remember being so mad! I wasn't fat but my mom and the doctor put me on a special diet. They wouldn't let me eat anything. So I went to my friend's house and ate whatever I wanted to. Then, my mom found out and told everyone that I snuck food. It made me want to eat more!"

"Okay, that's a good one," I wrote down some notes. "When else did you not feel loved?"

"My dad would say, 'Lillian, you don't have to have seconds.' Meanwhile, my sister who was so skinny--- I hated her, would get to eat pudding, cake, ice cream, pork chops. And they made me eat salad. I hated it. It was so unfair!" Lillian said.

"What other time did you not feel loved?" I asked.

"My grandma offered me money to lose weight. I didn't even want her money," Lillian was really crying now. "I don't want your money if it means that you don't love me as I am."

"Okay, and what time in your life or with who--- did you not feel important?" I moved on the second question.

"Um," Lillian stopped crying to think about it, "Oh! I started losing weight in high school and it was great. I was seen as pretty," Lillian waved her hair. "I got to go out with all the popular guys. I felt important, then. But it was like, I was dating them to show my mom that I wasn't fat anymore. To show everyone that I wasn't the fat girl and that..." she sniffled. "To pretend that the fat girl didn't exist anymore. But I still feel her inside of me. She was always so afraid to be discovered. Like, one day, someone was going to find out that deep inside, that I'm really fat and I'm not important or loved or accepted."

Yes! ==Lillian got to her master mask or the one who rules all her other masks. The name of that mask is, "Fat Girl Lillian."==

"So, Fat Girl has been dating all these guys. She goes out with the friend zone guys so that she can feel loved. She goes out with Alpha Male to pretend to others that she is not fat," I said. Lillian nodded. "The real Lillian has yet to date anyone, but Fat Girl has been dating all these guys." I paused.

Lillian sort of melted. "Everything I do, I do it as Fat Girl! If I'm not feeling thin some days, I won't go out. I won't go out if I think my outfit makes me look fat. I can't NOT wear make-up when I see people. If someone even mentions that they think I look big, I lose all my confidence. FAT GIRL RULES EVERYTHING!"

"So you're hiding from her, as well!" I pointed out. "You are wearing a mask to protect the real Lillian from Fat Girl. When Fat Girl shows up to date a man, where does the real Lillian go?" I asked.

"She's nowhere!" Lillian said. "She becomes a slave to whatever Fat Girl wants. If I feel great, but Don says I look fat---- then I immediately go into Fat Girl mode and change my outfit. It doesn't matter what the real me thinks or wants or feels. It only matters what Fat Girl wants."

"Why?" I ask.

"Because she's so sensitive! She can't get her feelings hurt. She can't be seen as fat. She can't let anyone know what her body looks like underneath the clothes and the make-up."

"Okay, so let's make a new column called 'Fat Girl.' And instead of writing down what Fat Girl is like, we are going to write down how you relate to Fat Girl," I said.

The first thing we wrote was, "Slave Lillian," who does whatever Fat Girl dictates. We found out that Fat Girl was not a shameful, embarrassed, shy and overweight person. She was a powerful and controlling behind-the-scenes force. Lillian constantly bought Fat Girl new clothes to hide her weight. She acted as Fat Girl's bodyguard and personal secretary, as she ran errands for Fat Girl's insecurities at inconvenient times. Lillian also missed out on a lot of opportunities, because of Fat Girl.

"How you do feel about Fat Girl?" I asked Lillian.

"I am afraid of her," she answered.

"Why?" I asked.

"Because if I don't do what she says, she'll get angry and tell everyone that she is really my mask and that I AM FAT GIRL," said Lillian.

"And then you won't be loved or accepted," I said. Lillian nodded. "But it isn't the real Lillian who needed that in the first place. It was Fat Girl who wanted to be loved, so you---- as Lillian, set up Fat Girl with all these friend zone guys. Fat Girl needed to date alpha males so that she could feel important."

"What does Fat Girl want?" I pointed to the section in Lillian's chart that said,

"Intentions."

"She already gets everything that she wants!" complained Lillian. "She is a spoiled brat who has never heard the word, 'no.' She pretends to be vulnerable and like a little girl, but she's not. She controls everything."

"What does she want?" I asked again.

"She wants to rule my life!" said Lillian. "I want her gone! I want to get rid of her. I don't need her anymore!"

"She will leave when YOU no longer need her anymore," I responded. "What does she want? What does the Fat Girl inside of you want?" Lillian just stared at me. We were so close to the answer. I said, "She wants to be free." Lillian's eyes were full of tears. We wrote on her chart, "In order for the slave master to be free, she must set her slave free. In order for the slave master to be truly free, she must be forgiven by her former captive slave."

"If you can forgive her by thanking her for teaching you what you need and want from a relationship with your real self---- then she can finally leave," I said.

> *The real Lillian has never gone out on a date. She has been dating men her whole life through the mask of "Fat Girl."*

INTENTION [or

fat girl everything she wants
fat girl is everything ERRIN should be
pretends to be vulnerable
fat girl is sure of herself
fat girl has never truly heard the word 'no'

I WANT TO BE FREE!

In order for the slave master to be free she must set her slave free
In order for the slave master to be truly free she must be forgiven by her former captive slave

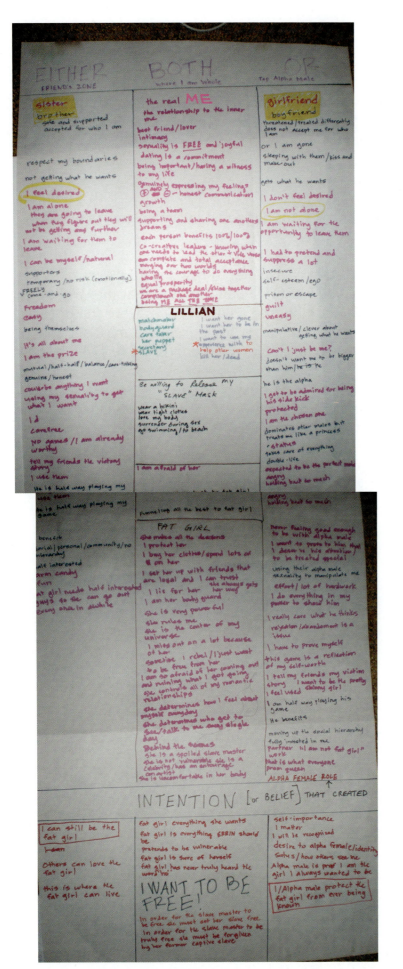

In order for Lillian to be free of her mask, "Fat Girl," she has to forgive herself for enslaving her life to the mask of "fat."

She was hiding behind her fat and using her fat to allow others to feel safe.

Friend zone guys felt loved by Fat Girl. Fat Girl made alpha males feel important.

Meanwhile, both Lillian and her mask of "Fat Girl" wanted to be set free from protecting each other.

Fat is Lillian's agreeement to protect men from feeling unloved or unimportant.

"Example of another man chart"

Girlfriend	Glass Wall	Home/ Social Acceptance	Mentor
sweet fantasy life, but they don't believe I'm real or allow me to become real	They don't include me in their real lives, ask me to hang out with their surf buddies.	They want me to be their perfect wife, less than, supporter, caretaker	father-figure, older, more experienced, controlling
vacations, not at home	gazing at him with "the boys" living their "real purpose" in life while I'm on the sidelines	Game: using me to make themselves feel normal, accepted or loved	landlord, alcoholics, men with no family around them
Mistress, 2ND OR 3RD CLASS	bikini model, dessert, SUPERFICIAL	Men who don't fit in	
		Wife, care-taker, BURDENED	daughter, LESS POWERFUL not capable

(capitals are how this makes me feel)

My masks that I put on or roles that I play when with men.

How men use me to feel loved, accepted, normal or compensate for their own faults.

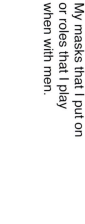

Men

As soon as I started to realize the "masks" that I play with men, all the men in my life including father-figures, landlords and teachers began funneling like ants into their appropriate categories.

THE MAN CHART

Third Session:
Creating a Body Chart

When Lillian released her mask as "Fat Girl," she stopped believing that she was "Fat Girl" underneath her disguise as the normal everyday Lillian that everyone else sees. Psychologically, Lillian was no longer living as "Fat Girl."

If she chose to be "Fat Girl," then she was conscious of when, why and how. She could choose to have fun behaving as Fat Girl or just drop the routine. But now, she would never be Fat Girl again and not have awareness around it.

I think that we cleaned out Lillian's "belief layer" in terms of how she operated as Fat Girl. In each overview chart, we usually lay out 4 layers:

- Spiritual
- Beliefs
- Emotional
- Physical

We changed Lillian's belief from, "I am secretly fat," to "I am not Fat Girl. I was her slave and now that I have forgiven her and released her as my slave master, we are both set free."

Fat Girl was no longer part of Lillian's mentality. She was only a memory. But the actual "fat" that Lillian accumulated from living as Fat Girl remained. We were going to trouble-shoot this fat, next.

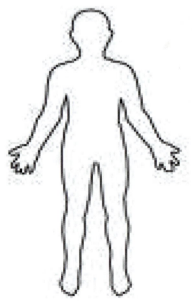

Step 1: Draw a picture of your body

We got out 2 huge pages of newsprint (18 inches high by 24 inches wide). We taped them together and I asked Lillian to draw an outline of her body---- like how a forensic detective would outline a dead body with chalk.

She drew her head, hair, arms, moderate sized breasts and then this tire-shaped lump around her torso. "What's that?" I asked.

"It's my love bump, like love handles?" she explained. "My midriff section is where all my fat is," she grabbed the skin on her waist. She continued to draw long thighs and legs.

"Okay, label each of the body parts and describe each one to me," I said.

Step 2: Label each body part and describe its function

"Uh, what do you mean?" she asked.

"What's this?" I pointed to her head.

"It's my face," she said, matter-of-fact. I noticed that Lillian didn't say "brain" or "skull." She didn't emphasize the importance of thinking or how smart she was, the function of her head was to show her face---- or to show her beauty.

"Okay, label it as 'face.'" I said. "What kind of energy do you hold in your face?"

"I have smooth silky skin, but some acne."

"What does it mean to have acne? Is it just a pimple and no big deal? Or does it attract energy from others when they look at you?" I asked.

"It means that I'm not healthy," she said.

"It means that you don't believe that you are healthy? Or others will perceive you as not healthy?" I asked.

"More others, than myself," she surmised.

"So external appearance is a reflection of inward health," I suggested, reading her energy. "The condition of your skin tells people the value or worth of your body's beauty?"

"My acne is an indicator of my internal health," she summed up.

"Okay, let's write down 'skin.' Then, put that it is an indicator of internal health which equals people's value or worth of your beauty," I said.

==Skin = health = other people's value of my beauty==

"What does your hair mean to you?" I asked.

"It's my power and part of my identity," she said.

"How so?" I asked.

"Well, it used to be really long, but I cut it when I joined my company because I thought it would make me look older,"

> *What is the function of each body part?*
>
> *What kind of psychic, spiritual or emotional energy is stored in each body part?*

she said. I gave her the marker and she wrote down, "length" on her chart with longer meaning, "little girl," and shorter meaning, "woman." In essence, it determined her position in the world.

"What about the color?" I asked.

"I used to bleach it but it made it look too platinum and stringy," she said and paused.

"What does stringy mean to you?" I asked.

"Like the little girl again," she said.

"What about the color now?" I asked.

"I think the natural color actually gives it more dimension and volume," she said. "The bleached hair-do got a lot of attention, but not the kind that I wanted." Here again, was a theme of Lillian's which was "attention." She added, "It's one of my natural features that works for me and that I don't have to resist, unlike other aspects of my body."

"So hair…" I was trying to sum it up, "has an overall function of what? What is the purpose of you having hair?" I asked.

"To be prized." We wrote it down on her chart.

"What about your arms?" I asked. "What function do your arms serve for you?"

"I don't ever think about my arms. They're okay," she said. "They carry stuff for me. I communicate with my hands. I use them to groom myself."

"Do they have any aesthetic value?" I asked.

"No," she answered.

"So if something doesn't make you more beautiful, you don't value it as much?" I asked.

"Yeah. If it doesn't affect how I look--- in terms of my body, then I don't really think about it."

"What about your blonde hairs on your arm?" I asked. "Because that affects how they look."

"That's the one thing," she said. "I shaved them once and I didn't like it. It made me feel vulnerable."

"Lillian's Body Drawing"

Skin: public admiration

Acne: indicates when I am being mean towards myself

Hair: identity, degree of power, position in world

Shoulders: confidence

Breasts: how I open myself up to the world

Arms: carrying things

Stomach: controls my life

Belly Button: indicates how fat I am or how much I agree to heal others

Thighs: only function is to exercise

Legs: power

Back: support

Butt: fun, friends

"What's wrong with that?" I asked.

"I felt like I have no protection against the world. I really felt naked without hair on my arms."

"So, naked is a bad thing?" I said.

"I hate being naked," she said.

"Why?"

"Because it means that I'm being judged." We wrote down nakedness = vulnerable = judged on her chart.

"Let's talk about your shoulders," I pointed to her drawing. "What function do they serve?"

"They help to balance and stabilize me," she said. "When I push them back and have better posture, it means that I am more confident in my abilities. When I slouch, I'm not feeling well."

"What about your breasts?" I asked.

"They are definitely tied to my confidence," she said. "It's a big part of my self-expression. Because I am not afraid of showing cleavage, like how I'm afraid of showing my tummy."

"In a way, it's how you open yourself up to the world," I say. I didn't sense sexuality in Lillian's breasts as much I sensed her openness to connecting with others. "What about your stomach?"

"Ugh. Yup. My stomach. This is the problem area, right here," she waved the marker above her chart. Lillian couldn't really think of anything to say about this area except for that it was "fat."

I had to help her brainstorm. So I said, "This area is where all your major organs are including the heart--- because they are sandwiched right in between the lungs. But it does not include the reproductive organs, the brain or the voice." I wanted her to think of the symbolism of this area. It did not incorporate intellect, communication or sex. It did, however, include love, digestion and nurturing the self.

Front side of Lillian's body:
How others saw her
How others placed a value on her body

Back side of body:
How she saw herself
How she valued herself

Fat:
Her agreements to heal others. The measure of her humanity.

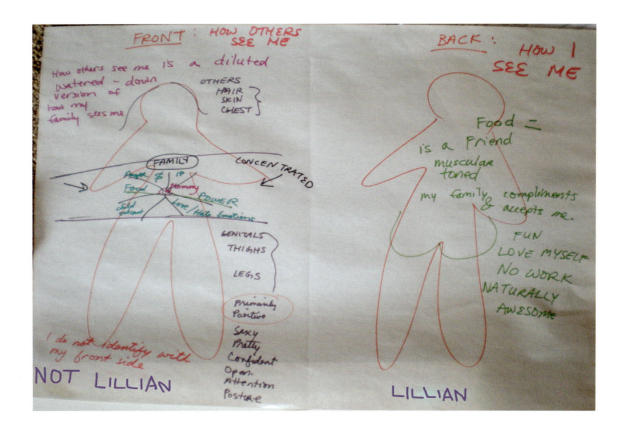

"Yeah, so what?" Lillian was not impressed.

"This area primarily breathes, feels love or hate, digests nutrients and keeps you alive," I said. "In and of itself, it is primarily a living breathing being."

"Okay," she jotted it down on her chart.

"We're not done yet," I said. "What purpose does your stomach fulfill for you?"

"It doesn't have one," she insisted.

"What about the belly button?" I pointed to the dot on her drawing. "Why would you draw a circle for it if it has no meaning? It must mean something."

She sighed, "It marks the center of my body. It lets me know I'm still human and normal because it's there."

"Okay," I said. "In a way, it's sort of the keeper of the stomach territory because it's the only form of human consciousness in this area, seeing how you don't give much love to your tummy area."

"Sure," she responded.

"How does your belly button feel?" I asked.

"Lost. Confused."

"Why?"

"Because he is hidden inside all this blubber!" she held her fists into the air.

"What function does he serve besides reminding you that you are human?" I asked.

"He's the indicator of my weight loss. Because when he is more visible, that means that I'm thinner," she said. I noted to myself, that the belly button was really an indicator of how human Lillian is. We are going to return back to this stomach area in detail in the next chapter.

"What about the thighs? What function do they serve as part of your body?" I asked.

"I don't like that area," she said. "They rub together and jiggle. But they are strong and I use them for exercising."

"Okay, and what about your legs?"

"I like my legs," she said. "They are long and I've always gotten compliments on my legs. I don't mind showing them off."

"What about your back?" I asked.

"You know what?" she said. "I love my back. I think it looks toned and sleek. I also love my butt. It's the perfect size and I never have to do anything to maintain it. It's perky and has a nice rump shape to it."

"Great. And what kind of energy is stored in those areas?"

"Fun, carefree, effortless and happy," she answered.

When we hide our fat:

Think of it like Cat Woman who has to hide her secret identity from men. She can't let them find out that underneath the "nice chick" persona, is an independent selfish bitch with claws!

Lillian's fat is her dark side. It holds secret powers: anger, power, control, rebellion and pure self-acceptance. It is her femininity which does not bow down to any man. But it also does not trust or relate intimately with them, either.

Step 3: What kind of "model" is your body?

We talked about:

1. How does each body part look?
2. How does each part of your body feel?
3. What kind of emotions do you have around that part of your body?
4. What memories or history does this part of your body contain?
5. How much do you value this part of your body?
6. Why?

When you do your own body drawing with some conscious thought and intent, you will begin to see a "model" emerging. I've had clients who've designed their bodies simply to seek revenge on men, as sexual weapons or others who primarily "mother" others. What you want to do is look at all the themes that keep repeating themselves. For Lillian, those themes were:

- Value (aesthetic) vs. no value (functional)
- Positive attention: being admired
- Negative attention: feeling vulnerable and naked
- Confidence and degree of power in the world

For the first theme, I asked the question, "How do you treat body parts that have no aesthetic value?"

Her answer was that she didn't pay any attention to them, at all. They were simply "there."

"What about body parts which are very aesthetic?" I asked.

Being honest, she perked up and responded, "They get all the attention!"

"From who?" I asked.

"From everyone," she said.

"Even yourself?" I asked.

"Sure," she answered.

"Okay, so the parts of your body which have great value to you are those which reflect and express your beauty. Everything else is not so important," I said.

> *What body "model" have you created for yourself?*
>
> *How is your body designed?*
>
> *What is the purpose of this design?*
>
> *For whom, is it designed for?*

"Yeah. Pretty much," she agreed.

"Value is assigned to your body based on how good-looking that part of your body is," I repeated.

"Yes, it actually determines how confident I'm feeling, how fat I'm feeling, how vulnerable I am--- it's everything," she said, again.

"Okay, so this is our major theme right here--- that your body has no value unless it is aesthetic," I concluded.

"Yes, because I'm in the anti-aging business. Your looks determine your power. It's not just about sales, but ever since I was little--- this was reiterated to me over and over again. It's how people treat me, undeniably," she said.

"Keeping that in mind," I pointed to her chart, "which parts of your body have value to you and which don't?"

She looked over her chart and waved her hand over the midriff, "Everything except my stomach."

"Everything?" I asked.

"Everything else is presentable..." she thought about it, "if I have the right make-up and clothes on, for that day."

"Everything on the front side of your body drawing is DEPENDENT upon whether or not you have make-up on and the right kind of clothes. What is make-up, Lillian? What is clothes? Aren't those the outer layers of who you PRESENT yourself to be?" I said. She nodded. "Aren't those masks?" I paused. "Which mask are you wearing when you put make-up on?"

"I guess, Little Girl Lillian," she hypothesized, "who has to look pretty so that others will do her favors or come to her rescue."

"Which mask are you wearing when you put exactly the right outfit on?" I asked.

"Definitely, Fat Girl," she said.

"Then, when does anyone ever get to see the true Lillian without her masks?" I asserted.

> *"Billboard Lillian's" body is a billbaord.*
>
> *It says, "Look, but don't touch."*
>
> *It says, "My fat is an object of your lust and desire. You can't have it."*
>
> *Like a billboard, it promises and withholds at the same time.*

Lillian looked down, "When I get out of the shower, I don't look at myself in the mirror naked."

"But you said you loved your back-side," I inserted.

"I can look at my back. I love my back. Just not my front," she admitted.

"Lillian, you don't own the front side of your body. Look at your chart," I pointed to all our notes. "The front side of your body is OCCUPIED by all your masks. Here is Fat Girl," I pointed to the tummy. "Here is Little Girl Lillian," I pointed to the hair. "Here is Sheep Lillian," I pointed to the slouching shoulders. "WHERE IS THE REAL LILLIAN?" I asked.

She pointed to the back side of her drawing, to her butt and to her back. "I'm here," she ran her hand down her spine. "I only take up the back side of my body. I let everyone else--- my mom, my dad, my sister, my alpha male boyfriends, all of them---- tell me what I should look like, how I should dress, basically how valuable I am based on how beautiful I look."

"So the front side of your body does not belong to you," I reiterated. "And what did all these people who you've been wearing all these masks for--- what did they tell you about the front side of your body?"

"That my legs are long and lovely. That my chest is nice. That my face and hair is nice. My arms are okay--- but my stomach is fat," she said.

Lillian began by telling me that these are all the things SHE thought about herself. Now, she was realizing that this was really what everyone else thought about her.

"And how do you dress?" I pointed to her outfit.

She sort of just looked at me with this honest stare, "I always wear short skirts and show lots of cleavage, but I always cover up my tummy." Lillian dressed like a billboard: to get attention.

"You display only the parts of your body that make you feel powerful--- those which are considered beautiful, valuable or presentable by others," I said. "In essence, you are a billboard. ==You are purposely displaying your body as an act of rebellion against those who called you fat for the past 18 years==, since you were 7 years old."

The major mask which Lillian wore on her body was called Billboard Lillian. Her body was a billboard used to entice and make men "look," but in reality--- she never offered them anything sexual in nature. She liked to make them want her, but then she wouldn't deliver the "touch." She tortured them by how she dressed. She enjoyed the power. They responded eventually, by tagging her in anger. They hated being teased. Lillian always walked away secretly satisfied, but on the surface, confused as to why they did not see her as an intelligent and respectful human being. It's because of the game she played with her outfits. Her semi-revealing clothing made men treat her like her mask--- as Billboard Lillian.

"This is Billboard Lillian," I pointed to front side of her body drawing. "It's not the real Lillian," I pointed to the back side of her body drawing. "You only own and occupy the back side of your body. Everyone else, all the spectators of your body--- determine how the front side of you will look and feel."

==The front side of Lillian's body (indicator of weight loss, external is a measure of internal health, degree of power in the world, confidence) is HOW OTHERS SEE HER. The back side of Lillian's body (fun, welcomes touch, perfect size, toned, looks good in anything), is HOW SHE SEES HERSELF.==

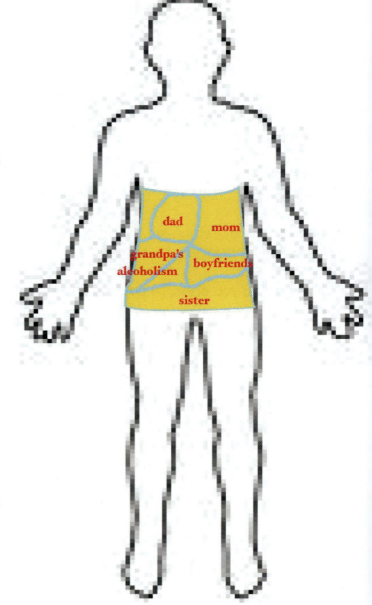

Why does Lillian use the front side of her body like a billboard? To punish those who have called her "fat" her whole life. To make them want her, so that she can withhold the "fat body" that they denounced in the past. In essence, what she is doing is displaying the "fat girl" as an object of lust and power--- rather than as an object of rejection or of being unworthy of love.

Her "Fat Girl" mask became an object of desire, when she presented herself as Billboard Lillian--- wearing clothing which revealed the parts of her which were considered beautiful. The way she dressed promises sex. But the way she acted, withheld it. It's a game of "look, but you can't touch" that incited anger in men, but gave her control over her fat.

Lillian would not have designed her body as a billboard unless she herself was expressing anger. My next question was, "Who are you angry at? Who do you want to punish?"

Step # 4: What is the motivation, motor or "engine under the hood" that drives your body model?

Looking at her body chart, it was clear that anger was expressing itself through her midriff. When Lillian had those horrible memories of her mother fasting and dieting for her or of her going to her friend's house in 3rd grade to gleefully pig out--- we wrote down on the chart right on top of her tummy, "Diet and exercise are a prison. Fat is a crime."

The prisoners of war inside of Lillian's midriff fat were her family and her ex boyfriends.

She was using her fat to protect her anger. She could eat and store fat, thereby never having to digest the anger--- and never having to give up food as power and a rebellion against her P.O.W.'s.

She could "store"= those emotions inside her fat, instead of setting both her prisoners and her fat, free.

All Lillian wanted to feel when she was a child, was that she was a normal kid who was healthy and care-free. In her rebellion, she ate to punish her mother. She also ate to tell herself, that she accepted and loved herself regardless of how others saw her. It was a form of self-acceptance. Later, as she got older and learned how to use her both her sexuality and fat as a form of revenge against men who found her attractive--- food became a source of power.

And in my mind, both her anger and her sense of control or power--- were stuck in her midriff. And she was using her fat to protect her power and her anger.

"You've got some prisoners of war in your midriff, Lillian," I told her. "Whenever you got angry at someone, you literally ate them. You ate them and stored the fat inside your midriff. You are storing your anger against those people inside your tummy fat."

Lillian thought about it, "My tummy feels like a prison of fat to me. And you are saying that I have prisoners inside this fat? That's why I need the fat? To keep them captive so that I can be angry at them for as long as I stay fat?" I nodded. "Forget that! I want them out."

"Then, you have to release your anger against them. You have to set your prisoners free."

Fourth Session:
The Psychic Core of Body Fat

I am not a personal trainer, a sports doctor or a nutritional counselor. What I am, is a psychic. When you eat food, I don't measure the grams of fat or carbohydrates. I don't gaze at your metabolism or calculate your age versus genetic health dispositions.

I take a psychic guess at how long you are going to stay fat or thin, why you are that way and the relationship it has to your food. It's never about food. It's almost always, usually, about emotions.

If you eat a hamburger when you are angry and you eat in order to relieve that anger, then I don't think you are eating a hamburger. I think you are eating your anger. I call those, "anger calories." Unfortunately, no amount of running or jogging is going to remove those anger calories from your gut. Because "anger calories" don't stick to the physical layer of fat surrounding your gut. They stick to the emotional layer of fat surrounding your gut.

Emotional calories stick to your emotional body. You must do emotional exercises to remove the fat. If you consume "anger calories," then your workout consists of releasing anger--- however you choose to do that.

This obviously presents a problem. I have a client who has been eating emotionally for 25 years. She was clinically obese when I met her. She tried every diet fad and aerobic exercise in the Northern American continent. But as soon as her husband died and she went into uncontrollable grief, she dropped 45 pounds in the first 6 months. Her weight continued to recede and after several years of not being able to contain her grief, her rage, her pain and her loss---- one day in the mail, she received a notice from her insurance company. They were offering to pay for a gastric bypass surgery, a $30,000 operation. After the surgery, she went on to lose 60 more pounds. When we start the ball rolling, the universe steps in to help us out. In essence, you just have to be willing to release your emotional fat. If you can't do anymore, your spirit guides will do the rest. In this case, her guardian angels sent her a free surgery.

Why do we emotionally eat? There are two types of emotional eaters. One type eats for the satisfaction of the emotion. They can't digest their emotions in any other way. So they eat them in order to experience the emotion. Alcoholics are great examples of this. They seem hardened, sort of like their livers, and for some reason, they can't freely express or experience their own deep-seated feelings. I know a lot of them say that alcohol is an "escape," but the reality is that it plunges them into the depths of their shadow side--- sometimes, a rather lovely and lonely, sad song or aria of their own soul. In this case, alcohol is being used as a vehicle for the drinker to get in touch with his/her emotional being---- which is not accessible to them, sober.

This is called addiction. While a lot of people dump on addiction, when you are psychic, it is a fascinating and noble endeavor. For you are risking pain and self-defeat, you are destroying parts of your health temporarily in order to brave seeing your emotional side. You are exploring the world of your own dark shadow. It is quite a journey. I have a personal experience with alcoholics, living in Hawaii. Many indigenous people drink and then start "channeling" their history of cultural genocide. So alcohol can also be a vehicle of experiencing the collective body of emotion--- for your family, tribe, nation or humanity, in general. There's danger and potential violence involved with addiction. But you can also see its appeal.

Power is power. Period. You can use it for dark purposes or for light purposes. One is not better than the other. Because eventually, all comes back to balance. The more dark you are, the more potential you have for increasing the "light" within you. The more of a light being you are, the more potential you have to attract that degree of darkness from others. As a healer, I will tell you---- my power to heal is born from my willingness to destroy. I am not afraid to enter into my client's darkness. Therefore, I have the ability to see the glory of their light side. We must have both. In fact, we all do.

The second type of emotional eater is one who is avoiding emotion. But I am going to go so far as to say, that they are avoiding the emotions of OTHERS, not their own emotions. They are trying to keep others from feeling sad, horrible or guilty---- so they eat FOR them.

==I am going to call this kind of eating, a "healing agreement."== For Lillian, she never judged herself, even as a child, for being chubby. She inherently loved herself and her body for what it was. But when her mother brought her to the doctor at age 7 to discuss her weight "problem," Lillian couldn't help but want to protect her mother from the "shame" of having a fat daughter.

Most healers have the gift of empathy. They can feel the feelings and emotions of others. So when Lillian's mother felt shame, so did Lillian. But Lillian was not feeling her own shame--- she did not have any shame around her own body. ==Lillian was feeling her mother's shame. And to heal her mother's shame within herself, Lillian ate. She ate in order to make her mother's shame feel better.==

Lillian ate in order to heal her mother's shame. She ate in order to heal her father's embarassment. She ate in order to heal her sister's loneliness. She ate in order to heal her boyfriend's insecurities. She ate in order to protect these people from their own emotions.

In fact, UNLESS YOU ARE EATING IN SHEER JOY, THEN YOU ARE NOT EATING FOR YOURSELF.

Extreme hunger counts as joy. Because you are happy to eat when you do. But the question I ended up asking Lillian was, "When do you eat for others and when do you eat for yourself?" Because she constantly ate when she was feeling the emotions of OTHERS and trying to heal their emotions within her own body. She rarely ate when she was not healing or protecting others from their emotions. In fact, when Lillian was happy and carefree--- being her normal grounded self, she rarely ate at all. When she did, it was usually something healthy and not the greasy food she chose to eat when she was feeling her mother's shame.

Releasing the P.O.W.'s of Fat:

"Are you ready to release your P.O.W.'s of fat?" I asked Lillian.

"Yeah!" she was excited.

"Let's say you are eating fast food," I said. "If you eat it in anger against your family, then you are eating anger calories. Anger sticks to your gut. Why do you need to eat something that will stick to your gut? Because you need to create a wall of blubber." I pointed to her body drawing where she wrote in "walls of blubber."

"You have a prisoner of war inside your gut, called your mom. You need the walls of blubber to keep your mom safe. You want her to be safe from feeling the emotion of anger.

"P.O.W. stands for power. Eating and food is your power. You can use it to control your mother's anger, as it exists in your body. In this case, you eat heavy greasy food. This blubber hides your mother's anger. Look at your chart." I pointed to where Lillian wrote down that her belly button was hidden in the blubber. "You are helping your mother hide from her own anger, by eating fast food."

"I get that I eat fast food when I'm angry at my mom," said Lillian. "I get that I'm hiding my anger underneath the fat. But how does that help heal my mom?"

Lillian ate fast food and heavy grease to build walls of blubber that would hide her mother's anger.

Lillian ate carbohydrates, oatmeal and bread to comfort her father's shame and embarassment.

Lillian ate sweets like chocolate and sugar as love for her sister's loneliness.

Lillian ate protein and beef to give nutrients to her grandfather's frailty due to his alcoholism.

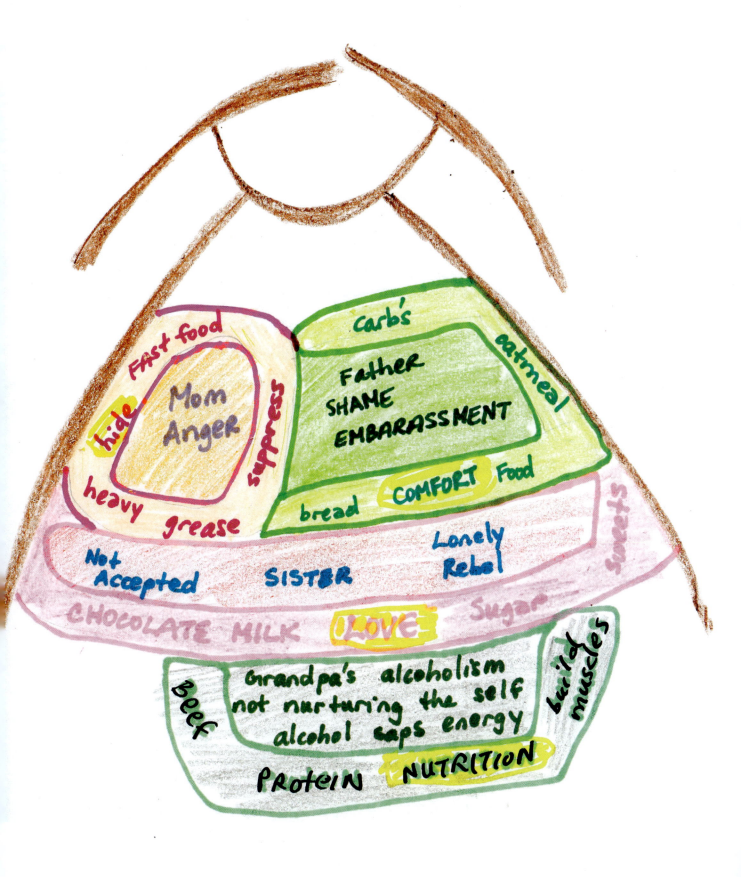

The way in which we heal others emotionally, is that we eat FOR them and not for ourselves. This is how Lillian's midriff fat was divided among those whom she was keeping safe from feeling their own emotions. Lillian ate to nurture her P.O.W.'s of fat.

Step 1: What kind of calories are you eating?

I said to Lillian, "If you eat fast food when you are in a mood to indulge, then you are eating indulgence calories. Is there any P.O.W. in your midriff that requires indulgence?"

"My sister," said Lillian. "You know what part of me is my sister?" she pointed to her body drawing. "The love bump. The fat I have here is just when I am indulging in food. My sister is in there because I indulge for her sake. She is always on some kind of diet or cleanse and I wish she would just lighten up! Sometimes, I just want to tell her to come out and party with me, to have fun."

"Great." I continued, "If you eat fast food for convenience, then you are eating convenience calories. Is there anyone in your life that requires you to be convenient?" I asked.

"My sister. I run all her little errands for her," Lillian waved her marker.

I went on, "If you eat fast food to feel better because you are feeling sad, then you are consuming sad calories. Why do you need sad calories? Which P.O.W. in your midriff needs to feel safe from feeling sad?"

"My mom," said Lillian. "I don't want my mom to feel sad."

"So you eat and create a wall of blubber to keep you mom safe from feeling sad," I said. "You eat sad calories that stick to your gut."

I went on, "If you eat fast food in celebration, then you are eating celebration calories. Are there any P.O.W.'s who need to feel safe from celebrating?"

"Maybe my sister," said Lillian. "She's so serious."

"So celebration calories stick to your gut a little bit, but probably not that much," I added. "If you eat fast food in total joy, then you are eating joy calories. Those calories NEVER stick to your gut," I concluded.

"Basically, you are going to say to yourself, 'All the fat in my gut is not food or calories. It is built from

> *FAT = EMOTIONS*
>
> *WORKOUT = RELEASE THE EMOTIONS*
>
> *THE WORKOUT COUNTERACTS THE EMOTION.*
>
> *BECAUSE THE FOOD DIDN'T PUT THE FAT THERE.*
>
> *SO DIETING WON'T REMOVE THE FAT.*

emotions. My fat is not hamburgers or grease. My fat is anger, sadness, convenience, etc.'

"Why do you need to intake emotional calories? To keep your P.O.W.'s safe from feeling their own emotions. You are not eating. You are nurturing the emotional well-being of others. OR you are keeping those whom you love from feeling upsetting emotions. You are protecting them by eating. What a simple and easy way to gain acceptance, love and friendship. Just EAT!"

Instead of confronting those people and illiciting some of those emotions, Lillian just ate the emotions. She said, "This week, my business was rocky so I ate because I felt despair, emotional, anxiety. I wasn't mad at myself for it. That was what I needed to take care of myself. What kind of calories were those?"

"Those were 'taking care of myself' calories," I said. "Do those kind of calories stick to your gut?" I asked.

> *FAT= HEALING AGREEMENTS*
>
> *LILLIAN'S WORKOUT=*
>
> *NOT HEALING OTHERS,*
>
> *NOT GIVING A RIP ABOUT MAKING THEM FEEL SAFE*

She considered, "Not really."

"Give me a number on a scale from 1 to 10, with 10 being the calories that stick the most to your gut. How does 'taking care of yourself' rank?" I asked.

"Probably a 2 or a 3," she said.

"And how do you burn those calories off?" I asked. "What type of activity does it take to burn off 'taking care of yourself' calories?"

"Just breathing!" she said.

"So those are really temporary calories," I said. "They slough off easily. How do you determine how fast these calories melt? If you no longer need to feel safe from taking care of yourself, these calories melt fast. But if you constantly feel like you are not taking care of yourself, those calories have to stay. In this case, Lillian, you are your own P.O.W. because you need to feel safe."

=="Hunger" is not about food. It's a need---- emotional and spiritual.==

==When we carry others needs for them, we eat and grow fat to nurture their needs inside of us.==

==We pretend to be fat to make others feel safe.==

Step 2: Give a number rating to each of your calories

Lillian and I made a calorie chart titled, "What kind of calories stick to my gut?"

We gave each emotional calorie a nickname and a number rating. Then we asked:

"What emotion do I feel when I eat these calories?
"How long or how much do these emotional calories stick to my gut?"
"What activity burns all of it off?"
"How long does it take to burn off these emotional calories?"

Number 1, easiest calorie to burn off was called, "Sugar." Lillian ate these calories when she was happy or feeling love. These calories burned instantaneously and the activity it took to burn them off, was just the beat of her heart.

Number 2, second easiest calorie to burn off was, "Nutritional." Lillian ate these when she was feeling well, healthy, in control and balanced. These calories were used immediately and were burned off just by breathing. It took a matter of minutes to burn these calories off.

Number 3 calories were named, "Band-aide." They were eaten when Lillian needed to take care of herself. They were burned off while she was sleeping. I asked, "How long do you need to sleep in order to burn off these calories?" She replied, "About an hour."

Number 4 calories were called, "Fiesta." They were eaten in celebration and gluttony. They were burned off by "waiting" for 3 to 4 days.

Number 5 calories were the "Lone Ranger" calories. Lillian ate them when she was lonely. It took her one long bike ride of about 2 hours to burn those calories off.

Number 6 calories were "Little Miss Lillian" calories which were eaten when she felt lost and confused. They stuck to her for 3-4 days of walking, doing pilates and working out with friends.

Number 7 calories were the "Rebel." She ate them in frustration and anger. She surmised that those calories have stuck to her gut for the past 18 years. The only thing that burned them off was self-help CD's, inner work and running at the beach.

Number 8 calories were, "Victim Story." This was when Lillian felt sad or depressed. She said that these calories can stick to her for several months. The only way to burn them off was to get connected with the people around her. The "emotional workout" was being in consistent friendship.

Eating

> "HUNGER" IS NOT ABOUT FOOD. It's a need —
> EMOTIONAL AND SPIRITUAL.
> When we carry others needs for them, we eat and grow fat to nurture their needs inside of us.
> <u>I pretend to be fat to make others feel SAFE</u>

Rating Scale: What kind of calories stick to my gut?

IDENTITIES ↓

Emotional Exercise

NUMBER RATING	EMOTION	HOW LONG MUCH DOES IT STICK TO MY GUT	WHAT ACTIVITY BURNS ALL OF IT OFF? (workout)	HOW LONG DOES IT TAKE TO BURN OFF?
1 sugar	comfort love happiness joy	it doesn't	my heart beat/no effort	instantaneously
2 nutritional	healthy well in control balance	used immediately	breathing	minutes
3 band aide	taking care of myself	very temporary	sleeping	1 hr
4 fiesta	celebration gluttony	minimal	waiting	3-4 days
5 lone ranger	loneliness	very temporary	one long bike ride	2 hrs
6 miss Errin little girl	confused lost wondering	3-4 days	walking + BLT class workout w/ friend(s)	2 sessions
7 the rebel	frustration anger rage	16 yrs	inner work/ running at beach	2 runs or 1 good counsel session
8 victim story fat	sadness depression	months	communication get connected be around people	friendship consistent relationship
9 small	despair hopelessness	18 yrs	reading feeding my head w/ inspiration	1/2 day
10 alpha female	stress anxiety fear	7 months	anger saying no putting Errin first	5 episodes each lasting couple hrs-3 days

THE WORKOUT COUNTERACTS THE EMOTION

THE FOOD DIDN'T PUT THE FAT THERE SO DIETING WON'T REMOVE THE FAT

FAT = EMOTIONS
WORKOUT = RELEASE THE EMOTIONS

THE "REAL SKINNY" LILLIAN'S WORKOUT:
NOT GIVING A RIP ABOUT MAKING OTHERS FEEL SAFE

Number 9 calories was, "Snail," which represented her belly button. She ate these calories when she was in despair and hopelessness. These calories have stuck for 18 years on her gut. The activity that burned them off was reading and feeding her head with inspiration. If she did this for half a day, those calories would start burning away.

Number 10 calories were called, "Alpha Female." They were eaten in anxiety, stress and fear of abandonment. Whenever she ate these calories, they would stick for 7 months--- because that is how long it took for her to break up with her last boyfriend. The workout to burn these calories off was anger, saying "no," and putting herself first.

Step 3: Fat Melting

We had been talking about eating emotional calories on a daily basis and how long those calories stuck to her gut. But what about the "fat" that was already on her midriff?

"Angry fat" came from eating anger calories without doing the workout that burned off anger. On Lillian's chart, she listed this activity as doing inner work and running at the beach.

Likewise, "sad fat" came from eating sad calories and not burning them off through "getting connected" to the people around her. "Lonely fat" came from eating lonely calories without doing the activity which releasee loneliness. "Victim fat" came from eating victim calories and not being in consistent friendship which helped pull Lillian out of her victimhood.

Fat accumulated when the emotional calories were not burned off by the "emotional workout" which released that emotion. It had absolutely nothing to do with diet and exercise, unless you were actually eating food calories. Meaning, eating food for the sake of eating actual food and not the emotion that the food helped you to hide or experience.

How fast does angry fat melt? That depends. For Lillian, it depends on how long she wanted her prisoners to feel safe from feeling angry. How fast does sad fat melt? That depends on how long Lillian wanted her prisoners to feel safe from feeling sad. Lillian said that she was done protecting her mother from feeling sad. She wanted that P.O.W. out of her midriff, now!

I rebuffed her, saying, "You've kept your mom safe for 18 years. If you set your prisoner free after 18 years of buffering her sad feelings for her, are you going to be anxious or worried about her? You are releasing your mother from a cushioned, sound proof blubbery jail (your own body) into a rough world where they are going to accuse her and humiliate her for…"

I had to check my notes to see what I wrote down. According to my notes, Lillian's mother used to humiliate her for being chubby. "For being chubby," I said.

"My mom is not chubby," Lillian said, "but it would devastate her to go out of the house with bad hair."

"Do you want your mom to be taunted when she goes grocery shopping for having awful hair?" I asked.

Lillian laughed at first, "It would serve her right."

"What if she started to cry and really felt bad about getting older?" I asked.

"No, I wouldn't want her to feel sad," said Lillian.

"If you don't allow her to feel her own sadness, then you are protecting her from feeling sad. In essence, you are healing her from her sadness. You are accepting her 'sad fat.' This is not your fat, Lillian! This is your mother's sadness. Do you want to carry her sadness for her--- which is the same as carrying her sad fat for her?" I asked.

"No," she said.

"Then, you have to allow her to feel her own emotions. You have to be okay with watching her cry and letting her feel sad, without trying to heal her. You can support and encourage her. But you cannot empathize in a way that makes you absorb her sadness into your own body."

Lillian sighed. I added, "If you want to burn fat, you have to stop healing others. What about when your sister asks you to run her petty errands?"

"Sometimes I don't do them!" she congratulated herself.

"Give me an example," I held my hand out.

"Last week, she asked me to drive 2 hours out of my way to go pick up some legal documents for her."

"How did you respond?" I asked.

"I said I'd call her back and I never did."

"Okay, did you go eat fast food that day?" I asked.

"Yes," she said.

> *"Hunger" is not about food. It's a need---- emotional and spiritual.*
>
> *When we carry others needs for them, we eat and grow fat to nurture their needs inside of us.*

"How did you feel?" I asked.

"Confused. I was worried that my sister was going to backlash on me somehow," she said.

"Okay, that is an example of eating 'Little Miss Lillian' calories," I said. "The fact that you felt bad about not helping your sister is the same thing as taking on her fat."

"How is that?" she asked.

"Every time you heal someone, you are taking on their fat!" I said. "She wasn't asking you to run her errand. She was asking you to take her fat."

"How so?" Lillian was confused.

"She got you to act like Little Miss Lillian, one of your masks. The REAL Lillian would not have responded with confusion. She would have told your sister that you are not an errand girl. You have important things to do with your time. BUT you wanted to protect your sister from feeling desperate, so you agreed to heal her by pretending that you would run her errand," I said.

Lillian looked at me. I repeated it, "Every time you heal someone or protect them from having their own emotions, you are taking on their fat. Every time you are not being the real Lilllian and wearing one of your smaller Lillian masks, you are taking on someone else's fat."

"I want to release my P.O.W.'s!" Lillian pounded on her midriff.

"Then stop healing them!" I shouted. "Don't run your sister's errands. Let her feel confused as to why you are not being her sheep. Let your mom feel sad and don't try to lecture her at the kitchen table with all your self-help books. Let them fail or succeed on their own path. Why does how they feel have to be your fault? Why can't you allow them to be responsible for their own feelings, whether or not you agree to act like their sheep?"

"Because I love them," she said.

"That's not love. That's a healing agreement. Those are two separate things. I can heal someone whom I don't love. Let's say I'm a doctor and I do a surgery on you. I don't love you, but I agree to heal you for money. I can also love someone without healing them. I can love myself, more than I care about them not feeling bad. In fact, if they feel bad--- maybe they'll finally learn something about themselves. Maybe they'll stop asking me to be their sheep," I said.

Step 4: Ending healing agreements

My theory is that there is a part of Lillian, even as a 7 year old, who wanted to protect her mother from this abuse or this pain that her mother made up in her head--- that the world is going to torture the two of them for being fat. Her mother made up this collective identity for the two of them.

At this point, Lillian sort of lost her own identity. Instead of "me, Lillian" and "you, my mother"---- Lillian became "us, the fat ones."

So then, Lillian, having lost her identity, doesn't speak up for herself. She doesn't say what she really thinks or feels. She never has a strong opinion if it disagrees with others. "Yes yes yes." is okay. "No is no," is not okay.

Because of "us," the potential fat ones---- she took on the belief that, "WE HAVE TO KEEP OURSELVES SAFE from being taunted by the world."

In Lillian's mind, her mom is kind of nuts. No one is going to torture her for being chubby, okay? Let's get real. But just as a courtesy, she will protect her mom from this mythical "fat torturing world" by cushioning and buffering her from feeling:

- Angry
- Sad
- Harassed
- Judged
- Confused
- Lost

And how will she buffer her mother from feeling this way? She will eat her emotions for her. And store them in her gut and not release them for 18 years. Because once she releases that fat, she will release the emotions that the fat stores. And then her mother will feel all that crap.

==She'd rather just store it in her body like a bank account of terrible emotions,== to spare her mother from the "us" and "fat ones" identity.

What's going on? Lillian is allowing her mother to live in a FANTASY world where there are fat-torturers running rampant in the streets. Lillian would rather not speak up, not stand up for herself, not DISAGREE with her mother. In essence, DENY reality in order to keep her mother's fantasy in tact.

This fantasy of her mother is based on FEAR.

So the longer Lillian holds these anger and sad calories in her gut---- it starts to harden, petrify and turn into FEAR calories. Or "fear fat." So when she starts releasing her fat, she not only has anger and grief, she has all this fear as well. Where is that coming from? Her mom's fantasy.

Lillian is FAKING compromising and taking on the "us" collective "fat ones" identity. In reality, she preserved her own true identity this whole time. But in order to protect her own identity, she had to keep it secret. How did she do that? She put it in the BACK side of her body where no one could see it. She also kept quiet and didn't disagree with anyone, or else they'd know that the real Lillian does not have the "fat one" identity.

She had to convince everyone that she is the "fat one." She had to send the message, "Don't let anyone know that I'm not the fat one. Pretend that the real Lillian doesn't exist. Just put real Lillian in the back, there."

Remember Lillian's body chart where the front side of her body was public property? It was a billboard. But the back side of her body expressed her true self, it was fun and carefree.

To keep everyone thinking that she is the "fat one"(safe) and not let them know that the real Lillian, skinny as hell and with the spirit of a wealthy celebrity/philanthropist truly existed --- she had to step back and let "Fat Girl" date all these alpha males. Surely, these trophy boys would let everyone know that she's Fat Girl.

So now, we have new fat that we've discovered in Lillian's gut. We have "pretend fat." It's not really fat. It's just for show. It's just like the alpha males. The alpha males showed the world that Lillian was Fat Girl. The pretend fat shows the world that Lillian is Fat Girl.

Her ex boyfriend, Don, is not a real P.O.W.. She didn't really care about making sure he felt safe from feeling crappy. But she kept him as a pretend P.O.W. to fake out the other P.O.W.'s and make them think that she really is Fat Girl. She kept her pretend P.O.W. to make all her other P.O.W.'s feel safe.

She had one P.O.W. to make the other P.O.W.'s feel better. She was using her ex boyfriend to keep her mother's fantasy in tact.

Don is a pretend P.O.W.. The blubber walls of his cell are made of "pretend" energy calories. It is pretend fat. It's fake fat. It looks like fat, but it's probably water or air. Lillian needed that just to fake being fat. She kept it around like a convenient outfit.

So Lillian consistently PRETENDS that she is Fat Girl. She pretends to be fat to make others feel safe.

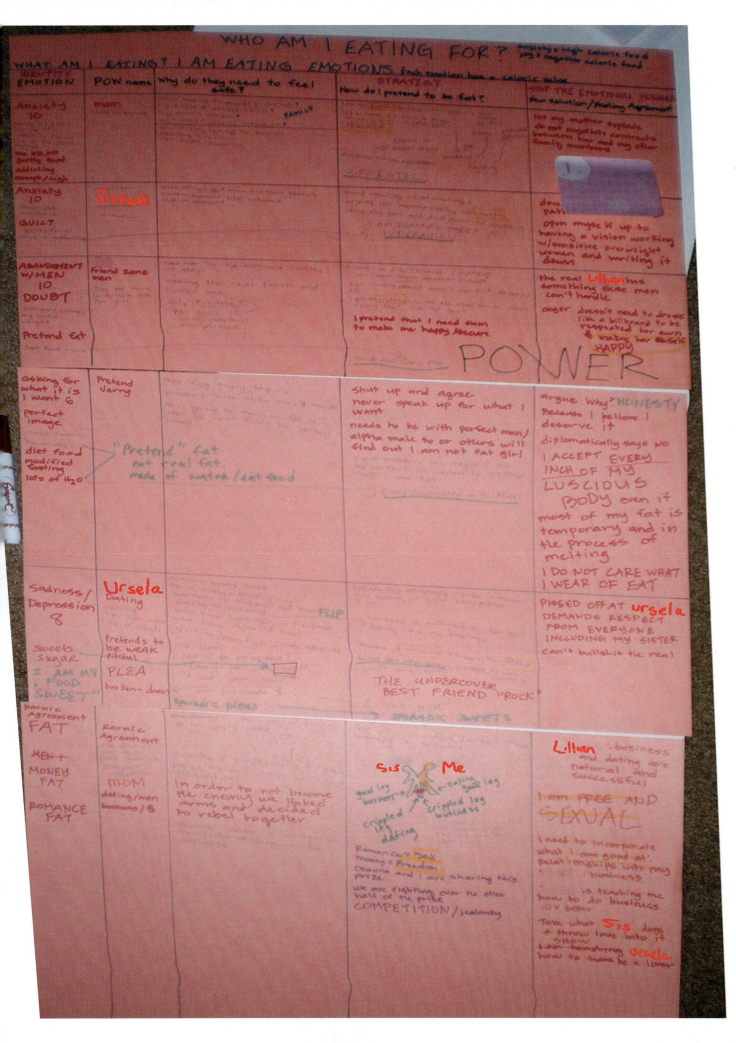

Fifth Session:
"Who am I eating for?"

This week, I wanted to talk about Lillian's diet. I asked her what she ate this week. She started talking about all the different kinds of foods she was eating: cereal, beef burritos, Taco Bell. Suddenly, I had an idea. "Let's do an eating chart," I said. "This is all going to make sense now that we have our emotional calorie rankings."

For starters, we wrote down the overall calorie rank of : anxiety equals high calorie food and joy equals negative calorie food.

Then we labeled the chart, "Who am I eating for?" Our subtitle was, "What am I eating? I am eating emotions. Each emotion has a caloric value."

We wanted to find out why Lillian was eating so much and how come she couldn't satisfy her cravings? Was there a solution to this problem?

Anxiety Fat

The very first thing we wrote on her chart was the emotion she was feeling this week. She said, "anxiety." We looked on her calorie ranking chart and anxiety was listed as a "10."

"Can you remember something you ate this week when you were feeling anxious?" I asked.

She nodded, "There was a whole lot. I ate..." she listed a number of junk foods. So I asked her to categorize or name that group of foods for me. She said, "Basically, the 'no no' guilty foods, high in fat and very addicting."

"Who did you have your major anxiety around?" I asked.

"My mom," she said.

"Why?" I asked.

"Because she sits there and stresses over the rest of my family. My aunt is sick, my cousin lost his job, my sister isn't talking to her again, my dad has high cholesterol. It's such a chaotic situation and my mom is trying to keep everyone at peace," said Lillian.

"How do you normally deal with that?" I asked.

"I'm the buffer between her and the rest of my family members. I calm her down. I just say whatever it takes to make her feel better. The same with my dad. I just try to take his perspective of things, so that he thinks that at least there is one person on his side," said Lillian.

"So you don't really speak your truth? You water down or sugar-coat your side of things, in order to make them FEEL SAFE from their own emotions?" I asked.

"Yeah," she rummaged through her charts. "Hm. That's the Little Miss Lillian mask not speaking her true opinion and always agreeing with others."

"What happened if you weren't the buffer? If you decided not to take on your mom's fat and you let her have her own emotions?" I asked.

"She would explode!" Lillian said. We wrote that on the eating chart, "Mom needs to explode."

"If your mother wants to release her own anger, she should explode," I said. "It will be healing for her to yell out what she really feels. But you are helping her hide her true feelings by keeping her from exploding. You are also carrying her fat for her because you want to heal her from exploding."

Lillian exhaled. "So I should just let my mom explode and not try to buffer it?"

"Yup, buffers need blubber to contain the explosive energy of 'anxiety.' You don't want the blubber anymore, do you?" I asked. She shook her head. "Then, you have to allow others to explode for themselves. Stop containing it for them."

She wrote down on her chart as a solution for "stopping the emotional hunger," that she would no longer negotiate contracts between her mother and other family members. She was also going to allow her mother to explode, if her mother needed to.

"How many times do you eat these guilty no-no foods?" I asked Lillian.

"Sporadically," she answered.

"And how often does your mom go into chaos-mode around your other family members?" I asked.

"Also, sporadically," she said.

"Do you see that what kind of food you eat, when you eat it and how often you eat it---- correlates exactly with the anxiety you are taking on for your mother?" I said. She nodded her head. "You are eating no-no guilty foods specifically to keep her safe from exploding."

"Ugh," she sat back.

WHO AM I EATING FOR?

WHAT AM I EATING? I AM EATING EMOTIONS. EACH EMOTION HAS A CALORIC VALUE

ANXIETY = HIGH CALORIE FOOD
JOY = NEGATIVE CALORIE FOOD

IDENTITY Emotion	P.O.W. name	Why do they need to feel safe?	STRATEGY: How do I pretend to be fat?	STOP THE EMOTIONAL HUNGER: Solution/ New Healing agreement
Anxiety 10 The "no no" guilty foods addicting escape	Mom (needs to explode)	Too much stress from other family members' problems. She has to solve things for everyone.	I am the buffer between her and the rest of my family sporadic	Let my mother explode Do not negotiate contracts between her and my relatives
Abandonment Doubt 10 fast food runs	friend zone guys men	keep men in the billboard fantasy of Lillian	I pretend that I need them to make me happy/ secure quick and easy	Doesn't need to dress like a billboard to be respected and make herself happy
Asking for what I want 6 pretend fat diet food lots of water	Alan, currently dating him	Pressure to be the perfect alpha male	I put pressure on myself to be perfect how often: whenever I am with men I like	Argue. Be honest Diplomatically say "no" I accept every inch of my luscious body even it most of my fat is temporary and melting.
Sadness, Depression 8 karmic fat sweets sugar	Ursela Sister sporadic pleas of "help!"	Horrible at dating good at business "In order to be loved by our parents, we each rebelled in only 1 area."	awkward at business successful in dating sporadic sweets, not eaten all the time	Business and dating are natural and successful Incorporate business into relationships: respect

Abandonment Fat

"What else did you eat this week?" I moved on.

"I went on these impulsive fast food runs," she said.

"Okay, what mood were you in when you did that?"

"Doubt," she looked at her calorie ranking menu. "That's a 10," she continued, "it was really about abandonment with men. You know, with my friend zone guys--- I never really got over why this one guy dumped me, Jim."

"Let's write that down on your chart," I pointed to the column labeled as P.O.W. and then asked, "Why would Jim need to feel safe from feeling abandoned?"

"Well, I'm the one who is afraid of that," she interrupted.

"I know, but my theory is that you are only pretending to be fat to make him feel safe. The real Lillian doesn't really give a rip about being abandoned. Your Higher Self never feels lonely or…" I look at her chart where she wrote in, "not good enough, over weight."

"So let's just theorize. Play my game, here. Why would this friend zone guy need to feel safe from being abandoned?" I asked again. "Let's say him and Fat Girl are at a restaurant. What would make him feel insecure about being left by her? Just make something up. Stretch your brain."

"Well, if she was dressed like how I normally dress with Jim--- like Billboard Lillian, all sexy with a short skirt, then he might be afraid that other men are looking at Fat Girl," she offered.

"Okay, why is that a threat?" I asked.

"Because Fat Girl doesn't really want to be with him. She's just using him to make other alpha males who might be looking, jealous. Actually, I've done that before," she admitted.

"Okay, so Fat Girl might run off with an alpha male if they are admiring her at the restaurant?" I said.

"Oh, definitely," she answered. "Also, when I'm acting like Billboard Lillian, I always please the man. I don't really let them see the real me."

"You also don't have sex with them," I said.

"Yeah, I don't let them see me naked."

"So, they really don't see the real you. They just see the billboard," I said. "Is this another way you make men feel safe from being abandoned by you?"

"Yes, I pretend like I'm happy and satisfied with them. Fat Girl never complains."

"So you are pretending to be fat, to pad their insecurities," I said. "How do these fast food runs feel to you?"

"Quick and easy," she answered. "Like my relationships with the friend zone guys--- quick and easy. I pretend to be Fat Girl and when I get sick of it, I leave them, one by one."

"What would the real Lillian do when she is faced with a friend zone guy who is feeling insecure about being abandoned?" I asked. "What would she do instead of maybe going out for quick and easy fast food?"

"She would…" Lillian thought, "think to herself that she has something that these men can't handle. She would be angry, too. She wouldn't need to dress like a billboard to gain their attention. She would make herself happy, instead of relying on them to take her out."

"Yes, she would own her power," I said.

Our game of flipping it around and pretending that the men were the ones who were threatened and not Lillian, worked. She realized that she didn't truly fear being abandoned. She was trying to prevent these nice guys from feeling abandoned by her. She could prove it, too--- because she dressed in a sexy way that made them feel more powerful and she never complained. But all along, she secretly knew that she was duping them and that she could leave them at her whimsy. She had to admit to herself, that she was actually more powerful than she was giving herself credit for. Her worry about being abandoned, was also an illusion.

She could prove that, also. Because she only went on these "quick and easy" fast food runs when she was trying to escape the reality caving in on her fantasy relationships with the friend zone guys. Lillian's emotional eating habits followed a pattern that we could trace, bite by bite, on her eating chart.

Pretend Fat

"What about this guy, Alan, I'm dating now? I really like him and I don't want to take on his fat or create another friend zone guy out of him. I want to have a genuine friendship with him and possibly, a romance," she said.

"Okay, when you think of him or when you are about to see him--- what do you tend to eat?" I asked.

"Diet food. I also drink a lot of water," she said. "Or I eat real cheaply, like not real food--- just low-calorie light snacks."

"What's the emotion when you are doing this?" I asked.

"I'm trying to have a perfect image," she said. "I feel like I'm pretending to be something I'm not."

"What do you mean?" I asked.

"I feel like I agree with him a lot because I don't want it to seem like I'm not happy. So, I never speak up for what I want. I wanted to ask him to hang out or to tell him, that I'm not comfortable paying as the woman. That most men, as a courtesy and respect to who I am, pay for the dates. But I don't want him to think that I'm a gold digger. That's not what I am. I just want to take things slowly with a guy, get to know him and when I'm good and ready, decide if I want to make an intimate connection with him. But it's so hard to just communicate that to him. I'm afraid that he's going to judge me."

"Which mask is that? Not speaking up for herself?" I asked.

"All of them," she replied. "But mostly Fat Girl. Because Fat Girl is the one who drinks all this water whenever she's around a guy she likes. She has to have this perfect image to hide who she really is."

"Okay, why would Fat Girl need a man to feel safe from having to be perfect all the time?" I asked.

"Ooh..." Lillian sighed. "If you're with a perfect woman, you need to be a perfect man?" she asked.

"Exactly," I said. "All these men are forced to wear a mask called 'alpha male' in order to measure up to the alpha female. That's a lot of pressure." Lillian nodded. "Fat Girl puts pressure on herself to be perfect, in order to pretend that she is fat." I motioned to her to jot it down on the eating chart. "How would the real Lillian act around Alan?"

"She would ask for what she wants," Lillian said it loud. "She would not be afraid of ARGUING. She would rather be honest and have a bond with this person, than pretend to be a billboard."

I read her chart from left to right. "So when you are around a guy you are attracted to, you want him to feel safe from having to pretend to be perfect. The way you do this is by pretending to be fat. You eat diet food and drink tons of water around him---- pretending to have a perfect diet. You are pretending to be fat, because only fat girls on diets eat that kind of cheap food. The real Lillian eats whatever she desires. The real Lillian would also speak up for what she wants, be honest and diplomatically say, 'no.' How often do you eat diet food and drink tons of water?" I asked, then pointed to her chart where it said, "Whenever I am around men whom I am attracted to."

"This pretend fat was created by eating diet food and drinking tons of water. It doesn't even seem like it should be fat because it's made up of mostly water. It's possible that you are bloated and feel fat, but it's not really fat--- it's water weight. It's water that is pretending to be fat."

Karmic Fat

"What else did you eat this week?" I asked.

"Lots of sugar and sweeties," she said. "I felt sad and depressed when I ate those, mostly around my sister, Ursela, because she's always acting miserable and desperate around me--- to get me to do her errands, for her. She acts like the victim and a martyr of EVERY situation. Meanwhile, she is a Blue Diamond making tens of thousands of dollars per month and I am a lowly Lapis, lucky to make $1,000 a month," said Lillian.

We wrote all these details into Lillian's chart. Then I asked her, "Why would Ursela need to feel safe from being depressed?"

"That's an easy one. She always single!" said Lillian. "She can never get a date. Meanwhile, I have tons of dates---- but I want business. Ursela has a lot of business savvy, but knows nothing about relating to men. I need more business savvy, but dating has never been a problem."

"So, you're opposites," I said.

"Totally."

"How did that happen?" I asked.

"Ursela is older, so she had to take the brunt of my parent's strict rules. My parents are really traditional and both Ursela and I, aren't. So Ursela decided that she was going to break my parent's rules when it came to business. She moved out of the house when she was young, got a job in sales which my dad hated the idea of and then made lots of money." Lillian continued, "I didn't rebel in terms of work. I rebelled in dating. I went out with boys, I did my make-up, dressed sexy, kissed them and spent all my time with them."

"How come you both didn't rebel in both areas: dating and making money? Why did you split it up like that?" I asked.

"We thought it would be too much for our parents to handle, so I guess we just naturally picked the one area we wanted to explore," she answered.

"So you guys made a karmic agreement," I said. "Kind of like a deal--- you rebel in work and I'll rebel in dating. And now, Ursela is successful at business and awkward at dating. You are successful in dating, but less successful in business."

"Exactly," said Lillian.

"This is karmic fat," I wrote on her chart. Under "Why the P.O.W.'s need to feel safe:" column, Lillian wrote, "In order to not become the enemy, we linked arms and decided to rebel together."

"So now what happens--- because you are working with your sister in the same company?" I asked.

"We fight over everything. It's a total competition. There's so much jealousy," she said.

"Yup. And so the fat comes from accepting this karmic agreement. You agreed to this, because the both of you wanted to feel safe from being unloved and rejected by your parents. If you let go of this agreement---- then what would be the consequences for the real you?" I asked.

"You know what? I don't have to be less capable in business, just so Ursela can be less successful at dating. I want both. I want to make money AND I want love. So I'm ditching this karmic fat, right here," she started drawing on her chart. "Ursela needs to incorporate some love into her business. I need to incorporate some business into my relationships. I need to speak up for myself, ask for what I want, rely on my intelligence and not my billboard body to get respect from others."

That was the solution to Lillian's hunger or urge to eat from depression and go get something sweet (or some love) to eat. The solution to melting the karmic fat, was to end the karmic agreement.

Sixth Session:
"What does it look like when I eat only for me?"

Lillian had been eating for all her P.O.W.'s, keeping them safe in her walls of blubber she purposely built from eating carbohydrates to comfort her father, sugary sweets to send love to her sister, greasy fast food to hide her mother's anger and protein to nourish her grandfather's alcoholic body.

"What does it look like when Lillian eats only for herself and NOT for any of her P.O.W.'s? Does she eat the same kinds of food, but with less or different emotions? Does she eat completely differently--- and change to a vegetarian diet?"

A lot of emotional eaters find that they don't even truly like or love their food. Food gives them guilt or relieves them of guilt. But the food itself, has no intrinsic value as food. Lillian wasn't appreciating the taste and color of her food--- or how it got from garden to grandma's hands to skillet to her plate. Her relationship with food, was taking food for granted and not loving it. She wasn't using it as a source of love and nourishment for her body. She was using it like she used her "friend zone" men--- quick and easy, convenient sources from which her ego drew on for energy.

Food is imbued with life when you choose to respect it, honor it and treat it as such. It can help you transform your body completely--- for better or worse. And it isn't the calories or the fat that counts. It's the way that you use food, that counts. It is only your intention that matters. Jesus turned water to wine, not because he wanted a higher alcoholic content in his beverage--- he wasn't thinking about the caloric intake or the potential liver damage. He had an intention to spread joy. He wasn't handing out liver-damaging potion. He was handing out joy. And when you drink in joy, your body expresses joy. It looks like joy. It feels like joy. It sends forth messages of joy.

You can do the same thing with water. Lillian was drinking tons of water dating men and gaining weight while she was doing it. Is water the answer or the problem? Is it the water? Or was it Lillian's intentions that created her "pretend fat?"

Lillian turned water into fat. A lot of you overweight people know how that goes. You can eat celery and gain weight.

Jesus turned water into wine. Same thing. Same process.

> *Lillina turned water into fat.*
>
> *Jesus turned water into wine.*
>
> *Same thing. Same process. But different intentions and therefore, different results.*

But different intentions and therefore, different results.

Your intentions determine the emotional fat stored in your body. Your physical body will begin to reflect those intentions once you change them---- because your body is a biological machine which spontaneously responds to your joy and almost always resists your negativity.

Step 1: Write a list of everything you ate last week

When I asked Lillian to do this, she started feeling depressed. "Just admitting this---" she referred to her list of foods, "I feel guilt. When I talk about it, I feel embarrassed."

"Why?" I asked her.

"Because this is such a private area of my life: eating. I feel like I'm being judged for not eating healthy."

"Who's judging you?" I asked. "Because it isn't you."

"It's my mom. I feel shameful for eating so much. I ate so much this week. I never felt that satisfaction that I was looking for. For that to be exposed, I feel vulnerable," she answered.

"You're healing your mother. Your mother is deathly afraid of losing Fat Girl. Fat Girl was like your mother's closest (CLOSET) and intimate friend since you were a little girl. Your mother needs Fat Girl to hide and keep her personal secrets for her. In a way, we all need our dark friends, don't we? We need the little black book of back-up sex guys we can rely on to boost our ego when we feel down. We need our party girlfriends to go out with and get blasted and drunk. Your mother had a wound that no one else would understand," I said.

"My mother's issue growing up was that she was scrawny and always wanted to gain weight and couldn't. Her father was an alcoholic," said Lillian.

"It isn't food for your mom," I said. "It's her body. Food is a way to control or maintain her body's nutrition. Alcohol saps nutrition and hydration from the body. Food is the exact opposite of alcohol. Her father was continually drinking. Your mother took it out on her own body and instead of using alcohol, she used food as the control source."

"How did my mother use food as a control source?" Lillian asked.

"She wasn't using food as the real control source. She was using her body as the control source. Food is just a representation of her body. She did not want to over-eat because she did not want her body to be visible. She wanted to stay invisible from this alcoholic father. She did not want to draw attention to her body and become the target of her father's wrath. Your mother NEVER WANTS TO DRAW NEGATIVE ATTENTION TO HER BODY."

"Lillian comes along and becomes invisible by occupying just the back side of her body. The front side of her body is a rebellion against invisibility---- it is her mother's nightmare, it is a billboard. But Lillian, in healing her mother's wound, decides to send the message to her mother that ATTENTION is not bad. This billboard gets love from men and outsiders and everyone in the public sphere. So her mother kind of heals a little bit. Attention isn't all bad. But in order to keep up this façade to show her mother that attention isn't bad, Lillian has to maintain the billboard 24/7 (24 hours a day, 7 days a week). The REAL Lillian who doesn't care about being fat or skinny or good or bad or has no real issues with attention---- just wants to USE attention to have fun.

"The real Lillian is bigger than other people's attention. The real Lillian uses attention as part of her Lapis Land goddess's tool box. The billboard Lillian is a victim to public attention. Why? To purposely send her mother the message that attention is not bad. It's a healing agreement. It's FAT.

"Your mother is using Fat Girl to hold the remote control that controls her eating or food OR the deeper core issue of her body. Fat Girl to your mother is alcohol to her father. She has managed to inherit the contrl issue and transfer it as fat into Lillian's midriff."

Sometimes, I talk to a client from a third person perspective. I told Lillian to write down a modified version of her original statement, "When I write down the food I ate this week, I feel ugly. When I talk about it, I feel embarrassed for my mother."

Her feelings about eating food, weren't really about eating food. They were about wearing the Billboard Lillian mask and healing her mother.

Step 2: Finding the right questions to ask about your food

The questions we came up with addressed the most significant patterns that showed up in Lillian eating habits:

1. What do I eat?
2. When do I eat?
3. Who was I with when I was eating?
4. How fast or slow did I eat?
5. What mood was I in?
6. Why did I eat or for what purpose did I eat?

We made a food chart listing each of the foods that Lillian ate. Then, we asked all these questions about each food.

We started with the first thing Lillian ate this week which was a La Salsa burrito. She ate it 8 pm with Alan, whom she was currently dating. "How fast or slow did you eat it?" I asked her.

"Slow," she said.

"What mood were you in while you ate it?" I asked.

"Back and forth. I was enjoying it, but I was also feeling guilty," she said.

"Why did you eat the burrito?" I asked.

"I was hungry, but it was more for social reasons. I wanted to bond with Alan," she said.

"Okay, so who did you eat the burrito for? Who did it benefit for you to eat the burrito?"

"Myself," she said. "I wanted to bond with Alan and that's what I got."

"Good, let's move on. What's the second thing you ate this week?" I asked.

"Trader Joe's beef burrito," she said.

"What time?"

"4 in the afternoon," she said. "I ate it really fast. I wasn't even hungry. I just ate it for no reason."

"What mood were you?" I asked.

"Lazy, lethargic, like I had no life force in me. After I ate the burrito, I felt guilty. Sometimes, I feel like I'm damaging my body when I eat for no reason," she said.

The words Lillian wrote down on her chart were: lethargic, no life force, damaging my body and healthy stuff. Ironically, "beef" is a source of protein. It is what we eat to add muscle and give us energy. It is used to counteract damaging our body. Body builders eat it.

> *Your body is the most honest expression of who you are.*
>
> *It is the most purest and innocent manifestation of our soul's core wounds, power, love, hate and total mythology of our humanity.*

The words that you use are very important. There are unconscious metaphors which you use in your speech. When Lillian said that she ate a La Salsa burrito to bond with Alan, I felt that she was eating for herself. But when she mentioned that she was eating a Trader Joe's burrito and thought about damaging her body, we paused for a moment.

Any time we come across a "blank" spot or a mystery in your chart--- where something is not absolutely clear and explainable--- we have to dig a little deeper. You should be able to read every single thing on your chart crystal clear from left to right, up to down; from your problem to the reason why things went wrong to its organic solution. A completed vision board makes sense when you read it, even if it is artistic or designed like a mandala.

"Who in your life can you describe as having no life force?" I asked Lillian. "You wrote on your chart that you were feeling lethargic and like you were damaging your body when you ate this burrito. I don't think those are the real Lillian's feelings. When the real Lillian eats, she always feels great. So who do these emotions belong to? Who are you eating for?"

"I don't know--- my mother?" Lillian takes a guess. "No, more like my grandpa."

"Yes, you're eating protein and beef," I said. "Elderly alcoholic Grandpa needs nutrients and to build his body back up. You are eating for him. This is genetic fat. Your mother agreed to heal his alcoholism by making her own body scrawny and invisible, to avoid his wrath. You hide your eating from your mother, as Fat Girl. Your grandfather is hiding his alcoholism by hiding his anger. You mother is hiding his alcoholism by hiding her body. You are hiding your mother's shame by hiding your eating."

"Blah," said Lillian. "Alright, the next thing I ate was oatmeal. I felt unsatisfied with what I ate prior. I think that 'emptiness' describes why I ate it."

Because Lillian took a break from work this week, she felt empty and that she didn't have a community or wasn't making any money. She was needing money, needing community, needing a connection to people and to her downline. She needed to feel like she was on her soul path.

I told her that, "Doing nothing, relaxing, deliberately NOT putting forth doubt energy or billboard energy into the world, showing up as the real Leader Teacher Lillian---- IS being on your soul path. It is active."

"It doesn't feel fulfilling," she admitted. Then realized, "I was disregarding that this was part of the path because I wasn't having any intense emotions in any way. It was really mellow. But when I took inventory of the week, I did end up making contacts and moving forward in my business. I felt more enlightened than drained."

Lillian's fat was reacting to the mellow, calm, ease of business and life. Lillian's fat was more used to the excitement, the drama, the kill, the seduction, the energy, the failure, the disappointment, the break-up and the make up---- all of the neon lights of her old billboard. All of a sudden, it was a calm summer breezy day at the beach and no alpha male was torturing her midriff. There was just no energy, no P.O.W.'s, it was so lonely, the prison was vacant and the fat was feeling empty.

So the fat was whimpering, feeling kind of unproductive and thinking, "It's so quiet around here. What is my function? I'm FAT. I'm supposed to be emotional. I'm supposed to have drama. I'm supposed to heal others. What am I doing? I have no purpose???"

Lillian was thinking and feeling the emotions of her FAT this week and getting confused.

Exercise: Talk to the fat

I pretended to be Lillian's fat. Then, the 2 of us (Lillian and her fat) had a conversation. If you are doing this at home, you have to talk to a pillow or a marshmallow. Pretend the pillow is your fat and it is talking back to you.

Fat: I feel empty and lonely. Can I have some carb's please? I need to heal someone. Hey, let's ask your mother to eat with us.

Lillian: No, no. No, no. This prison has been evacuated. We're making room for making love.

Fat: I don't want anyone to touch me, you know. I've been stuck in prison for 18 years. My hair is a mess. I'm jiggly. I don't really do any aerobics in jail. If I do, I eat donuts to make up for it. So, making love ---- OH! We can make love, sure! If we can turn it into a healing agreement and you can get me another P.O.W. through making love, then I won't be so lonely.

Lillian: Absolutely not. No. No. NO!

Fat: Fine, bitch. Get me some OATMEAL!!! You know what? I'm pissed. Let's go to Taco Bell.

Lillian: Fat, you know I love you. I've taken care of you for 18 years. And I don't want to break up with you. Let's BOTH change. Let's turn ourselves into "making love machines." Let's turn into smooth silky skin and muscle. Let's belly dance. Let's pole dance. Let's eat strawberries and cream. Let's let Alan eat strawberries and cream off of our belly button. Let's have FUN, Fat.

Let's let go of all that guilt and depression and loneliness. Let's have friends, not POW's. Let's have lovers. Let's have MONEY. Let's begin a different journey. Forget the prison! It's over. We're building a resort spa. And you are my BESTEST co-creative business partner. Together, we are going to build an empire for sensitive overweight women through my company.

When Lillian first tried to say NO and discipline the fat, the fat acted just like the 7 year old girl who had to sneak food to rebel against her mother. It rebelled against Lillian. Discipline, hard exercise and dieting didn't work for Lillian. Her fat was not HAPPY. She couldn't fight her own urges and her own body.

Your body is probably the most honest expression of who you are because it NEVER denies itself anything. That's why we have addictions. Because our bodies are the purest and most innocent expressions of our soul's wounds, power, love and hate. They embody the mythology of our life path. So we have to listen to our bodies. And we have to make better deals with them.

Lillian enslaved her fat and tried to discipline it through diet and exercise and always felt like she was withholding LIFE and JOY from herself. She was also withholding those good emotions from her fat.

The solution was for her to listen to her fat. What was it teaching her? Then she communicated with her fat without judging it, criticizing it, denouncing it---- but learning from it. Then her fat helped her to build a better life and person. To BE the real Lillian. To build an empire.

Purpose:

Lillian kept asking, "Why do I keep eating for others week after week? We've been building all these food and fat charts for me--- and I still keep picking up other people's energy and eating for them."

I remembered Lillian's lifetime goal, which was to help sensitive overweight women to be more happy. She not only wanted to succeed as a salesperson of anti-aging products. But she wanted to eventually earn so much money that she became also, a celebrity/philanthropist. She also wanted to have her own talk show. I said to her, "This is why every woman in America is going to identity with you. Because you identify with every woman in America."

My theory is that Lillian could eat whatever she wanted to without getting fat AS LONG AS SHE WAS EATING FOR HERSELF ONLY. But when we examined every morsel that she ate this week, we discovered on her food chart, that she was still eating for others. She had only 1 meal this week where she ate for herself.

In my personal opinion, Lillian was overeating for others. She was healing others. Meanwhile, she was starving herself. She was not feeding her own body. She was only feeding her fat. Meaning she was eating in order to feed her healing agreements --- to keep others safe from having their own emotions.

I wanted Lillian to eat FOR HERSELF. To stop starving herself. I felt that food-wise, she was anorexic in terms of feeding herself, even though she thought of herself as chubby. But she only owned or occupied the back side of her body---- because she hadn't built the front-side for vacancy for Lillian. She put in a prison for others to occupy. She was still building the walls of fat for these lost and absent prisoners.

I wanted her to eat for herself, so she could start building the walls of muscle for herself to occupy the throne of her body, which to me---- represents her future empire, with Fat as a co-creator of LIFE. With FOOD as a co-creator of joy.

Practical Application:

Lillian asked, "The pro-active approach to all this is to take inventory before I eat and double check if I'm eating for somebody else?"

I retorted, "Nope. The point is not to analyze every frickin calorie you're going to ingest. The point is not to think, dissect, gauge, measure, weigh or feel the calories or fat grams of each food you eat. The point is not to DO anything with your food. The point is to BE the real Lillian—the Lillian who is healthy, muscular, golden, tanned, toned and hot---- and then eat your food from that sexy place and you can do whatever you want.

"AS LONG AS YOU ARE NOT EATING FOR OTHERS and only eating for you. If it ain't sexy, it ain't food."

Bob Greene, who is Oprah's personal trainer, his approach is to measure all the calories and work out hard and compensate for aging metabolism. His approach works. His clients are thin. But I don't care if my clients are thin. I want them to be happy. Why? Because when you are happy, you are tapped into your true power. And at will, when you decide that you want to be thin OR fat, your body will magically change for you. Why? ==Because in Bob Greene's eyes, age and metabolism--- your own body is your enemy. And in my eyes, your body is your bestest friend.== And you don't have to fight it. You have to convince it to make love with you and have fun with you. And it will do whatever and whenever and however you want it to.

> *To master the physical, we must master the emotional. We must incorporate the spiritual. Why? Because all of Lillian's fat and everything she eats isn't fat. It's emotions. And her new beautiful body? Emotions as well. And when we incorporate the spiritual--- it becomes her empire. It is an expression of her power.*

Seventh Session:
Who am I feeling chubby for?

Lillian came back the next week, saying, "I want to know what's going on with my body. All I wanted to do was eat. This whole week, I have been feeling the complete opposite of what I felt before. I feel happy, more in balance and really chubby."

Who was Lillian feeling chubby for? Because the real Lillian didn't judge herself as being chubby or not chubby. She knew that because her body was a temple for her energy, it was completely and totally changeable by will. She willed it to look or be or channel a certain energy and it immediately responded to her. And others immediately responded back.

Ask yourself this question: "Am I truly feeling chubby for me? What would be the purpose of this? How do I benefit from feeling chubby? If it makes me eat healthier and go exercise, then that's great." Maybe that could be a benefit of feeling chubby. But there are also emotional benefits to forcing yourself to feel chubby. See, the real YOU, meaning your Higher Self never feels chubby OR skinny OR anything, but well being.

> *The fat that exists in America is not fat.*
>
> *It is our emotional well being.*

Your real self ONLY FEELS WELL BEING. If you are actually chubby, your real self thinks to itself, "Chubby is well." If you are skinny, your real self thinks to itself, "Skinny is well."

"Chubby" and "skinny" become characteristics of well being WHEN YOU ARE BEING YOUR TRUE SELF. Your Higher Self continually holds unconditional love for yourself EVEN, WHEN AND IF you are abusing yourself. It will still hold love for itself.

Let's say you are abusing yourself in some way. Let's say you are bulimic and you decide to go on a binge. While you are doing that, you have to put yourself into an "eating" trance so that you can gorge even when your body signals to you that it is full. You have to "override" the natural instincts of your body to stop eating and convince yourself that the eating is some form of "good" or that it feels great. It feeds your ego.

While you are doing this, your Higher Self will sort of "lift" out of your body. Literally, your soul hovers about a few feet above you, maybe even 50 feet or more if it really doesn't want to have the direct experience of you abusing yourself. And it watches from a neutral distance, thinking to itself, "Oh this state of abuse is temporary. She is just re-learning a karmic lesson about her body. So I'll hang out here and when she's ready for me to come back, I will."

Even as you are feeling horrible vomiting into a trash can, your Higher Self has love for you and will gently tell you, "It's okay, sweetie. You can vomit it all out. Don't worry. This is temporary. This is just another lesson you are exploring and re-learning about your body. Come on, hon. Let's take a warm bath and then go to bed. You've done a lot of exploring your lesson today---- meaning, you've done a lot of vomiting. So let's just take a break and rest."

In the mind of your Higher Self, there really is no reason to forgive yourself even when you choose to abuse yourself. Because there is no "negativity" in learning karmic lessons. It is just "learning." Binging and vomiting are just "exploring." Everything becomes part of your Divine Plan.

My point is that Lillian's Higher Self didn't really give a rip about being seen or feeling chubby, because there was nothing wrong with being chubby. Chubby was good. Chubby was cute. Chubby was real. Chubby was chubby. It had no negative connotation to it. So, if Lillian was feeling chubby and attaching a "bad" vibe to it---- why was she doing that? It wasn't for herself. Her real self didn't care about it.

==Who would care if Lillian was chubby? Who benefitted from Lillian being chubby? Who got a fringe benefit or ego satisfaction if Lillian felt chubby? Who was Lillian feeling chubby for?==

I'll give you a blatant example. Do you think that if Pamela Anderson was stranded in the Himalayan mountains for 14 years and only lived with gorillas, she would have an impetus to get silicon breast implants? Would that help her to survive the jungle or benefit her person in any way? No. But she lives in America and works in the entertainment industry. Who did you think she got those implants for? Probably for her target audience who buys the movies and products which she sells and profits from. True, they give her love and that feeds her ego.

But her Higher Self and her ego are 2 separate beings. They are not connected except that they both share her mind and her body. But even then, her body has a physical aspect to it--- the muscle and flesh. And it has a spiritual energy to it---- her aura, her ability to birth children and mother. Her mind has an ego aspect to it--- to gain attention, flattery and riches. And it has an evolved consciousness that rules it--- the woman who searches for her power and nurtures her young.

So her implants might have benefited her ego, but it did not benefit her Higher Self who thinks that, "Implants are well. No implants are also well. All is well." There is no judgment from the Higher Self. But there is also no benefit to the Higher Self. When we meditate and feed the soul---- there

> *Lillian's belief:*
>
> *I am willing to be chubby in order to be loved and accepted by the whole world.*

WHO AM I FEELING CHUBBY FOR?

I chose love over skinniness

Who am I feeling chubby for?	Why?	How does it benefit me/them?	How consequences of me not being willing to feel chubby?
Alan (man)	they can feel superior chubby girl is not a threat/desireable	they wouldn't be threatened by on lookers. chubby girl limits her options. I resist the urge to heal someone I love from feeling discomfort or pain.	what would be the consequences of me not being willing to feel chubby? I don't care that men feel threatened by my beauty. • Alan is uncomfortable • Break the land and connection for the night SOLUTION: I have to be ok with Alan not being ok.
Sister why would Ursela need me to feel chubby?	She feels successful not threatened. Skinness is a competition	I am the package without the fat if I am skinny Lillian has lost the war fat is the last battle. • when I feel chubby I am Ursela's number 1 sheep	I am the enemy I become a threat • She kills our sisterly relationship • Lillian now has the capability to make Ursela one of her own sheep. • She would make my work a lot harder for me I make BLUE DIAMOND
Mom (women)	I want to feel chubby so that women and my mother will love me	What is chubbiness? what dark secrets? Dark secrets am I carrying for other women? my mother's anger for her father's alcoholism. that she is carrying women feeling rejected by men. For younger more beautiful women like myself. I am not at threat and they are more likely to bond with me.	when a woman sees me she doesn't see my weight. They connect with my warm genuine energy.

Skinniness is not effort at a struggle at being happy myself.

Chubbiness is a struggle to keep others happy.

BEING HEALTHY

HEALTHY means that there is no such thing as fat or no fat there is ONLY alignment.

is lots of benefit to the Higher Self. But almost all material and ego needs are not beneficial to the Higher Self. They benefit the body, the ego and our survival.

So, Lillian's "chubbiness"---- just like Pamela's implants, benefited someone, somewhere. And it wasn't Lillian's Higher Self. Who was it? Why did it benefit them and how? These are the questions to fill in on her Chubby Chart.

First person to feel chubby for: men

First question: Who am I feeling chubby for?

Lillian had a hard time with this question, "Are you saying that I don't truly feel chubby?"

"Yes," I said.

"Okay, so when I was with Alan on Tuesday, I felt really chubby," she said.

"Yup. It wasn't the real you who felt chubby. You were feeling chubby for Alan's benefit," I said.

"Why the hell would I do that?!" she asked.

Second question: Why would men need you to feel chubby?

"Okay, answer that for me," I ordered.

"Uh? Um, I guess, chubby girls are not a threat to their power and masculinity because no one wants her and she is not desirable?" offered Lillian.

Third question: How would that benefit men for Chubby Girl to NOT be desireable?

"Men wouldn't be threatened by other more alpha males if I was chubby," she added.

I asked, "Who cares if people are looking at Chubby Girl? Are you saying that these men are actually Chubby Girl's second choice and that if she had options, she would leave them?"

It benefited men who were with Lillian for her to feel chubby, because then they wouldn't be threatened with her desirability to other males.

Fourth question: What would be the consequences of me not being willing to feel chubby?

I asked, "What would happen if you went out to dinner, looked hot and Alan was uncomfortable with how hot you look? What would the consequences of you not feeling chubby be--- on that particular night?"

Lillian thought about this one, "It would make Alan, my boyfriend, uncomfortable. For that night, it would break the bond and connection between us."

Fifth question: What is the solution?

Let's say, that Alan felt uncomfortable and that the bond was being broken between him and Lillian, because every man in the restaurant was staring at her hot body. So instead of shrinking and slouching to compensate for Alan's uncomfortably--- which is what Lillian would normally do--- meaning, she would try to heal Alan's discomfort and take on some of his fat---- so instead of taking on Alan's fat---- Lillian decided to NOT FEEL CHUBBY.

So she says to herself, "I'm not going to take on his fat. I'm not going to feel chubby. I'm going to sit here and own this. I am going to be hot and allow everyone to look at me WITHOUT FEELING insecure or chubby, EVEN if Alan is feeling insecure and chubby."

In order for her to not have felt chubby, she had to be OKAY with Alan feeling chubby or Alan feeling uncomfortable while she sat across the table from him and ate while everyone was admiring her hot body.

She would have to be okay with Alan not being okay. In other words, she had to NOT heal him. She had to resist the urge to heal someone she loves from feeling discomfort or pain.

We wrote that into her chart:

I resist the urge to heal someone I love from feeling discomfort or pain.
I am okay with Alan not being okay.

Do you see how Lillian felt chubby in order to make men feel comfortable, as well as be accepted and loved?

Second person to feel chubby for: sister

"Why would you feel chubby for Ursela?" I asked.

"To make her feel successful," said Lillian.

"How does weight or chubbiness show a measure of success? Why would you being chubby make her feel like a success?" I asked.

> *Being skinny is no effort at being happy, myself*

Lillian said, "Skinniness has always been a competition between the two of us, to see who looks better. Also, I feel like I'm the complete package without the fat. It's the one thing keeping me from having it all. Because once I'm thin, I would be able to make money, have a relationship and be confident. I would feel like nothing would ever hold me back."

Fat was the last battle between Lillian and her sister. She could win the war, if she were skinny.

Instead of finding a "solution" for the last column, we substituted the phrase, "How I chose love over skinniness." In each case, Lillian felt like she wasn't going to be loved by someone if she were skinny. So, we wanted to look at the consequences of her deliberately choosing not to feel chubby.

In this case she felt that if she allowed herself to be skinny in front of her sister, then she would feel like:

I am the enemy
I become a threat
She loses a sister and a friend because she can no longer treat me like one of her sheep
She kills our sisterly relationship

I asked, "How would that make you feel if your sister just cut you off?"

"Ambivalent," she answered.

"How so?"

"I would feel a loss, but then I would move on."

"It seems like you don't give a rip about what Ursela feels, but then why is she even on your chart? Why did we bother to write her name down, then?" I asked.

Being chubby is a struggle to keep others happy.

Lillian said, "I feel like I try to work towards a relationship and she keeps trying to be an imposing force on that. She will be nice when she needs something and then she goes and screws it up. I'm trying to have her in my life, still. I want to bond with and love my sister, not the bossy side of her. At one point, I wanted to bring my sister up to the Team Elite stage when I made Blue Diamond and thank her."

"Why are you willing to feel chubby for Deana?" I asked again.

"I want her to love and support me, when I win. I want her to feel like she won with me. I want her to have a little credit," said Lillian.

I said, "Your sister is not evil. But she is evil when it comes to you because she has forced you to be the sheep in this sister relationship. You have to be the sheep. When you are in the sheep role and she is shepherding you---- she has to act like the shepherd, in control, powerful and knows better than you. But when you pull yourself out of the sheep role and force her to treat you like a sister and not a piece of meat---- what happens?

"She breaks the sisterly bond and turns it into a competition. When you are the sheep (i.e. a piece of meat), the fatter the better. Because she owns you and she likes fat sheep. But when you are rival shepherd and you have fat sheep in your flock serving you hand and foot like she has you doing for her---- then she becomes oh-so-worried. Why? Because Lillian now has the capability to make Ursela ONE OF HER OWN SHEEP. Ursela is scared of her own slave. Because her slave knows the secret to the slavemaster's power.

"Lillian is an incredible threat to Ursela because she is her closest, most intimate friend and supporter. And Ursela constantly fires or screws it up or purposely sabotages intimate relationships---- because she is threatened or worried that her own sheep will turn on her."

Lillian was willing to feel chubby so that her sister would not make Lillian's work harder for her, since they work in the same company. When Leader Teacher Lillian chooses not to feel chubby for Ursela, she makes Blue Diamond.

Third person to feel chubby for: women

"I got really thin, one time in high school. I was starving myself. I remember being worried as my weight dropped, that other women weren't going to like me as much being skinny," said Lillian.

We wrote on her chart, "I want to feel chubby so that women and my mother will love me."

What was chubbiness in this instance? It represented dark secrets. What dark secrets was Lillian carrying for other women?

When Lillian brainstormed about it, she came up with:

My mother's anger that she is carrying for her father's alcoholism.
Women feeling rejected by men for younger, more beautiful women like myself.
I'm not a threat when I am chubby and they are more likely to bond with me.

Fat relationship:

will you love and accept me?

We then wrote down on her chart, "I am willing to be chubby in order to be loved and accepted by the whole world."

"If that is what chubbiness is--- then, what is skinniness?" I asked her to brainstorm again.

"A threat," she said. "It is the most desired trait of women because it has the most value placed upon it by society. It is one of the areas that we women tear each other apart, instead of linking arms. It is a huge way that we are judged first, by other women--- and then, by men. We care more about what another woman thinks of us than a man."

"What is the solution?" I asked her, continuing with our brainstorm.

"No effort," she said.

"What does 'no effort' mean?" I asked.

"It means that there is no struggle to just be myself," she said.

"Why are you not willing to feel skinny?" I asked her.

"Because being skinny means that I am not loved. I am an enemy. I am a threat. I don't identify with Skinny Girl. I would be leaving Lillian behind if I was Skinny Girl," said Lillian.

"The 2 choices you gave yourself were skinny and fat. You never gave yourself the choice of healthy--- whether you were chubby or not. You pitted skinny against fat and they were both enemies. In your mindset, skinny is being not loved, a threat. Fat is being loved and accepted even if you have to risk being hurt sometimes. It was a choice between not-so-bad fat and even worse, skinny."

Lillian relationship:

This is who I am.

Are you in alignment with me or not?

Skinny sucked. So we put in a new thing called "healthy"--- onto Lillian's chart.

What did healthy mean? Lillian brainstormed it as being, "Toned, muscled and athletic."

"Okay, but what does it mean in terms of relationships and being loved?" I asked.

"I will not be judged or related to just based on my weight. People will connect with my genuine warm

> *Healthy means that there is no such thing as "fat" or "no fat."*
>
> *There is only alignment.*

energy. They will be talking to my face and my eyes. They will be responding to my wisdom. They will not be staring at my weight or talking to my fat," she said.

LOVE relationships (include mother, sister, father, boyfriend, women and men) to Lillian was always a relationship between another person and her fat (weight, midriff, chubbiness and body).

Lillian's primary relationships have been whether or not people loved her fat or didn't love her fat. Whether they abandoned her fat? Or stayed with her fat? Whether they loved her regardless of her fat or didn't accept her without her fat. Her fat had all these family dynamics, boyfriend relationships and friendships with women. She related to love and relationship always through her fat.

"Right now, all your relationships are not really you and Alan. You and your mom. You and Ursela. It's your fat and Ursela--- meaning, Sheep Lillian and Ursela. Your fat or Little Girl Lillian and your mom. Alpha Female or hiding your fat or Skinny Girl and men. Your identity as a lover and a lovable person is always tied to how fat or how not fat you are," I said.

"Where and when you are 'healthy' has nothing to do with fat or weight. It's just the real Lillian relating to the rest of the world. In the realm of healthy, there is no such thing as fat or not fat. There is only alignment."

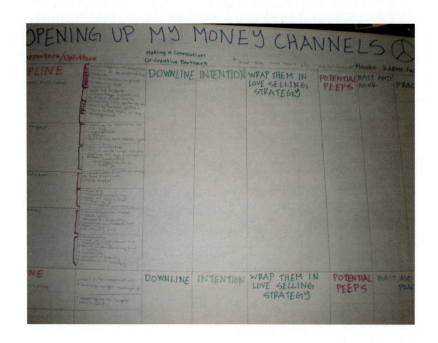

INITIATING A GROWTH SPURT

Top of the mountain:
achieving a goal
learning a lesson
spiritually evolving
becoming a better person

Many people climb the ladder or take steps one at a time, in order to reach the top of the mountain. The mountain represents your goals or achieving a spiritual lesson.

It can be a fast-paced tiring journey. It can be slow and methodical, without drama. But each step is a stepping stone to get to the top.

Others like to skip the whole stair-case. Instead, they prefer to fly up to the top by loading themselves into a sling-shot. Instead of stepping forward towards the goal, they seem to pull backward away from their goals. They create miserable negative experiences of what they do NOT want.

What they are actually doing is building momentum. Delving deeper into their negative beliefs. When they hate their situation enough--- they surrender and release all the negativity. Then, their slingshot propels them forward---- over people's heads and they land on the top of the mountain.

There are 2 ways to finish a growth spurt. You can climb steps. Or you can sling-shot your way to the top.

EXTREMELY NEGATIVE EXPERIENCE CAN CAUSE A FAST GROWTH SPURT AND RESULT IN EXTREMELY POSITIVE EXPERIENCE.

Lower than the bottom of the mountain:

difficult, horrible experiences

core negative beliefs

Eighth Session:
Emotional Meltdown
When my best friend, "Fat," leaves me

Where does your power lie? What do you fall back on when times get tough? Is it men? Is it food? Is it money? Is it your mother?

For Lillian, it was her ability to deal with any crisis, pain or EMOTION that came her way--- as long as she had the ability to eat for others. She could heal anyone around her who decided to "change" her force field or the natural aura of her well being, simply by eating.

Let me give you another example. Let's say your house is spic and span clean. You spent years cleaning this immaculate mansion of yours and then someone tries to step into that house with muddy shoes. You could get upset and start shouting at them, "Get out! Take those shoes off before you step foot in my house!" But if it is someone whom you love and you want them in your house because they have had a long hard day and need to rest---- you don't want them to feel judged for having muddy shoes. So what you do is stand there armed with your Lysol, Pine Sol and mop. Everywhere they trek in your house, you follow them and clean up after them. Problem solved.

==Only, instead of the proud owner of a mansion--- you are now, its maid.==

In order to keep her self-esteem clean and not let the way that others judged her affect her, Lillian's version of Pine Sol was food. She could keep others from knowing that their own self-judgments or their criticisms of her weren't going to hurt her. She was a trooper. She was going to be a cheerleader and a helper. She wasn't going to let them get her down. In the process of this, she became their sheep.

The person who relied on her as their #1 sheep the most, was Ursela, Lillian's big sister. Ursela needed Lillian to run petty errands, to complain to when she felt lonely and perpetually single, to clean up their shared office space, to valet park her car, to deliver documents, to be a secretary, psychotherapist, best friend and servant. While Ursela did not pay Lillian, the "promise" was that as a Blue Diamond in their multi-level marketing company, Ursela was going to help Lillian as a lowly Lapis climb the rungs of success with her experience and connections. That never panned out. After 9 months in the same company, Lillian never got promoted beyond her current status as Lapis.

In other words, Lillian was the proud owner of a mansion called her body. As a favor to those whom she loved, she agreed to store their "emotional baggage" in her mansion in the form of fat. Ursela would come by, drop off a load of fat or some big problem that she was going through---- and ask Lillian to "take care of it" for her. Lillian agreed to be a maid. In her own mansion! Also to store, maintain, polish and wax the fat of her guests and not even her own fat. Pretty soon, her mansion became permanently "chubby."

"What am I supposed to do?" Lillian asked me.

"Just say no." I sounded like Nancy Reagan.

"I can't," she complained.

"Do you wanna be fat?" I asked.

"No."

"Then, 'no' is your perfect answer," I said. "It isn't Ursela asking you to valet park her car, run errands and deliver her mail. It's Ursela asking you to take some of her fat."

"How is that?" Lillian asked.

"Every time you heal her, you take on some more of her fat," I say. "She's not asking you for a favor from one friend to the next. She's expecting you to be her hoe sheep who always bows down and answers 'yes.' She is your pimp shepherd and every time she orders you to bend over, she is dirtying your lovely skinny mansion with her emotional baggage fat."

"You know what?" Lillian's eyebrows raised. "I'm just going to avoid her."

"Then, she'll just leave her load of fat on your doorstep. She knows you are going to pick it up and clean it for her. You--- a maid," I said.

Lillian paused. "You're right," she had tears in her eyes. "I feel sorry for her."

I cleared my throat. "Lillian, how much do you make as a Lapis?" She didn't answer me. "About $1,000 a month," I answered for her. "How much does Ursela make as a Blue Diamond?"

"$20,000 to $50,000 a month," Lillian said.

"She's got you to feel sorry for her? What a scam."

> *Fat is a healing agreement.*
>
> *The healing agreement can be as simple as:*
>
> *I agree to carry your emotional baggage for you.*
>
> *Therefore, I will carry your fat inside my body.*

115

Keep in mind that I have spent 2 months with Lillian thus far and I have never taken on this tone with her. I had to prep this woman for 8 weeks before I could get her in the boxing ring. Now, I've trained her and I was putting her up for a fight.

I continued, "Your pimp shepherd isn't going to let her #1 hoe sheep, off that easily. You know, she is not going to let YOU just walk away from her. If you want to leave this fatty relationship with your sister, you are going to have to be strong. You must rise above her, ask HER to meet you eye-to-eye. Not lower yourself and hope that she leaves you alone. She is successful and a Blue Diamond for a reason. She knows what she's doing. You are a Lapis. Let's see what you got."

Lake Tahoe

Lillian went to a self-help conference sponsored by her company. There were a lot of New Age speakers and business people who were networking there. Her sister was also supposed to attend, but cancelled at the last minute and decided to leave town without telling anyone where she was going. Lillian ended up going to the conference, by herself. Before she left, she solidified a business partnership with a dermatologist, Dr. Susan.

They were excited to work with one another on a concept called, "Brains and Beauty." Dr. Susan would provide the scientific research behind anti-aging products and Lillian would run the demo's where women would receive complimentary facials. They had been planning on working together for weeks. For Lillian, this represented her "big break" in her company. Dr. Susan had a fine reputation and Lillian felt lucky to be chosen by her to be a sales partner.

Prior to leaving for Lake Tahoe though, Lillian's sister chummed up to Dr. Susan and started meeting with her privately. Lillian assumed it was just out of friendliness, as they are in the business of making quality connections with others wherever they go.

I also had a piece of advice for Lillian before she left. "I got a psychic flash," I told her. "I think you are going to have a fat abortion."

"What is that?" she asked.

"It's when you release a bunch of healing agreements, all at once," I said.

"Is it going to feel bad?" she asked.

A fat abortion is when you release all the psychic energy from your fat, at once.

It occurs when you decide to end all of your healing agreements.

"It's going to be a moment in time that is going to break your heart. ==You are going to realize how you have kept yourself from your own power,== this whole time. And you are not going to experience regret--- so much as love for yourself. You are not going to just think that you deserve more--- but you are going to KNOW that you ARE more. It is going to awe you how you could have lived your whole life not knowing this, before. People are going to immediately respond to the change in your energy. You are going to emanate the real Lillian. You will never be Sheep Lillian, again."

"Okay, good. Because I want this fat to drop all at once. None of this 1 pound here and 2 pounds there, kind of weight loss," she said.

"Yes, you will release all the psychic energy from your fat at one time. The purpose of sad fat was to keep someone safe from feeling sad. But if you release the sadness, there is no reason for the fat to hang around. Without a meaning to its existence, the fat will just fall away. Emotion put the fat there in the first place. Emotion keeps it there. But if you are no longer protecting someone from feeling sad, you release both the emotion and the fat which stored it," I drew the equation for her.

1st Phone call: Fat Abortion

At midnight on Monday, I got a call from Lillian. She was sobbing and dry-heaving, uncontrollably. I couldn't understand any of her words as she was screaming and choking on her own tears at the same time.

"I got this call from Dr. Susan. She just started ranting about how I am irresponsible, not capable, ripping into me and I am trying to ask her what is wrong… but she won't listen! She won't listen!" Lillian is hiccupping on her tears. "She keeps cutting me off and telling me her drama about how I'm too young and naïve to know what I'm doing. She's telling me I'm not a leader and I'm slowing her down."

"Wow," I said. "There was nothing about Dr. Susan that---- I mean, this is totally out of the blue, yes?"

"This was my big opportunity to work with her. I don't know what happened! She is just ripping me open. I gave her all my trust! I shared my DREAM with her and now she is yelling at me for no reason," Lillian was inhaling her sobs while she spoke. "It feels like knives are going through my back…"

"Interesting," I listened more.

"Then… she keeps promising me that she has a big project in the works, so big that she can't even tell me about it. She said that she already sees all the mistakes I'm making because she made them, too." Lillian made these weeping sounds. "I hurt so much. I feel like she's sliced me open from head to toe and she just keeps repeating over and over again that I need to LISTEN to my sister. That my sister is such a success and I'm a total failure and I need to take Ursela's advice..."

I wrote down on my notes, "Blackmail."

Lillian cried out, "She cut me open. I d-don--- I don't want her around. I can't see her. I am so clear. I need to get people who really love and support me. She is an extension of Ursela. She is fighting Ursela's battle and acting like a badgering prison warden to me. That is not okay. I get any charge on anything and she flips out on me. I am a person. I am an adult. I take care of what I am supposed to do. I can't get a hold of Ursela. She's out of town."

"Lillian!" I shouted.

"What---?"

"The fat doesn't want you anymore!!! Your very own blubber is evicting you from the blubber house. It thinks your body is not acceptable blubber material anymore. You aren't as blubber-friendly as you used to be, you skinny rich happy bitch! WHO ARE YOU to not host, grow and give birth to more blubber constantly? You are a blubber murderer! You deserve to die for the sake of blubber's longevity," I said.

==Lillian was blubbering about her series of verbally abusive phone conversations with Dr. Susan, while I sang in the background. Our dialogue went something like this:==

Lillian sobbing, "NOT EVEN MY OWN MOTHER TALKS TO ME LIKE THAT!"

"OH my god, you're way ahead of schedule. Psychically, I didn't see this coming until Wednesday evening. I thought you'd call me on Thursday morning, peaceful as a dead blue jay and tell me about the horrific night you had, and how the fat had aborted itself from your midriff---and here you are in the middle of your fat abortion, calling me and telling me how---"

"AND THEN SHE SAID THAT I WAS SLOWING HER DOWN. AH AH AHH... AND THEN SHE SAID THAT I WAS IRRESPONSIBLE AND I AH AH AH.. AH... AH... WASN'T... AH AH AH... CAPABLE AND..."

"You know how skinny you're going to be Lillian? Ooh, and you can buy new clothes."

"AND THEN SHE SAID THAT ALL I EVER DO IS SURR----"

"I knew it. That fat was the last thing standing in the way between you and your success."

"SURROUND MYSELF WITH DRAMA AND I AH AH AH... OH.. IT HURTS SO BAD... WHY?"

"You know what? Your sister brought out the big guns. You know she must have smelled success and money on you so bad that it brought her to this?"

"I CAN'T HANDLE THIS... AH AH AH..."

"I'm so impressed. No way your sister would go through this much tedious detailed effort to sway Dr. Susan and then get out of town at the same exact moment you were having your fat abortion. She definitely planned all this..."

"AH AH AH... AH AH AH... But I am not even making money yet, I am still a Lapis!"

"But she can smell the Blue Diamond scent on you. She knows that you are on your way up and she is going to nip it in the bud. The money must be really close, otherwise why would she feel so threatened for no reason?"

"This is ridiculous! WHY WOULD SHE DO THIS TO ME? I have only loved and supported her this whole time. It doesn't make sense."

"She... hey, hey! Get a grip. What are your spirit guides saying to you, right now?"

"I'm torn open. Is this the fat abortion?! Because AH AH AH AH..."

2nd Phone Call: I never want to date "fat" again

On Wednesday, I got another phone call from Lillian. This time, she not only had residual feelings of pain from the previous nights of abusive phone calls from Dr. Susan--- but she had calmed down enough to hear her spirit guides talking to her while she sat quietly, feeling sorry for herself.

"Dr. Susan decides to call my dad," she sighed. "She even called my other upline in the company to bad-mouth me."

"Ooh," I found that fascinating. This was soap-opera quality.

"The clearest thing that came to me from my spirit guides was to move out of my sister's office space, as soon as possible. The Nazis are Ursela and Dr. Susan. They want to strangle me," she said. "Then, I heard my spirit guides tell me that there is another local office I can work from and there is new support coming in for me."

"Okay, what other insight did you get?"

I had advised her to sit still in the moments of her greatest pain. To stop the crazy sobbing, while trying to observe herself from an omniscient 3rd person point of view. Like, you are neutrally watching yourself go nuts. In that quiet observation mode, you can begin to ask your spirit guides questions. If you sit still enough in the midst of your pain, you can even hear God talking to you. This was exactly what she did.

"She's been calling me every day and leaving messages. I feel like it's not her that's talking to me on the phone. It's my fat or it's Ursela. And when I respond back to her in my head, I'm not talking to Dr. Susan. I'm talking to the universe. I'm sending the Golden Money Chute in the Sky, a message. I'm not going to take it, anymore." I imagined her pointing her finger to the ceiling of her lodge.

"Now I'm in a bind. I have absolutely no desire to return to work," she admitted. "I'm not connecting with it. I just keep thinking that this is not what I want to do. I'm in the wrong profession. I'm so unhappy with it. I have been for 9 months. Who am I kidding? I don't want to be doing this?"

She continued, "I am beyond confused and in crisis. What is my other option? Is this just me going through a moment? Or me getting really clear and realizing that joining this company was all about Ursela and not what I really wanted?"

It was my turn to respond. I gave her a long response, prefacing it by telling her that this was what her spirit guides were saying:

"You are falling for Ursela's trap. She has successfully killed all passion or love or caring or any positive feelings you could possibly ever have for your company again. She wants you out of this business.

"This is similar to a real abortion. After you have an abortion, you don't want to ever date another man again. You don't want to see a penis, a condom, nothing. You are done. You will never make the same mistake again with a guy.

"In this situation, you had a fat abortion. You were healing your sister and teaching her a valuable lesson about relationships. She was the 'guy' in this case who screwed you over. She planted the 'seed' of this company into your heart and thought that if you ever succeeded in this company, she was going to take the credit for it- --- this is her baby, not yours, even though your success in this company was grown from your own hard labor and love just like a fetus grows inside a woman's womb.

> *Your enemy will always know you more intimately than your lover.*
>
> *Your lover only sees your strength. Your enemy knows that your greatest strength is also your weakness and a liability.*
>
> *Your enemy, like the universe, sees both sides.*

"Ursela could have used your dedication and loyalty to learn something about relationships, like how not to be a manipulative insecure boss. But instead, she decided to screw you over.

"Well, little did she know---- that you have a choice. You didn't have to be her sheep and birth this baby FOR her. You could just have a fat abortion. If you were to have continued doing this business under your sister's supervision, it would be like having her baby for her. She would have used your success--- like how a man uses your child, to blackmail and control you, forever.

"But before you even began building your business--- the universe forced you to miscarry. You aborted that seed. This week, you dropped all this fat. And the new baby and success you are going to carry forth into this company will not be shared by your sister. She cannot claim any credit for your success because you are still a Lapis.

"What Ursela is trying to do, just like the father of your aborted fetus---- is trying to get you to NEVER DATE ANOTHER MAN AGAIN. If he can't have you, nobody can. So he wants to kill your desire for dating, any hope for love, he wants to make sure you know you are worthless and think that you do not deserve to be loved.

"So Ursela has her 'gang' of upline (including Dr. Susan)--- she has even tried to rally your family against you---- which is, by the way, what abusive husbands do to their wives whom they beat, to try to destroy all love you have for this company and any hopes of succeeding in this business.

"Think of Ike and Tina Turner. Ike beat Tina to death for years and turned her children against her. He wanted to kill all desire she had for singing. But what did Tina do? She divorced him and walked away with nothing but her name. And what happened to Tina? What happened to Ike?"

Lillian calmed down at this point and responded, "That just turned the business around for me. I can finally understand why all my efforts with my sister and working side by side with her were getting me so down. I am pleased that the universe is working to protect my success from being associated with Ursela."

When Lillian is dripping fat, her enemy only smells "money." Ursela knows that soon, Lillian's discarded fat will make her into a Blue Diamond.

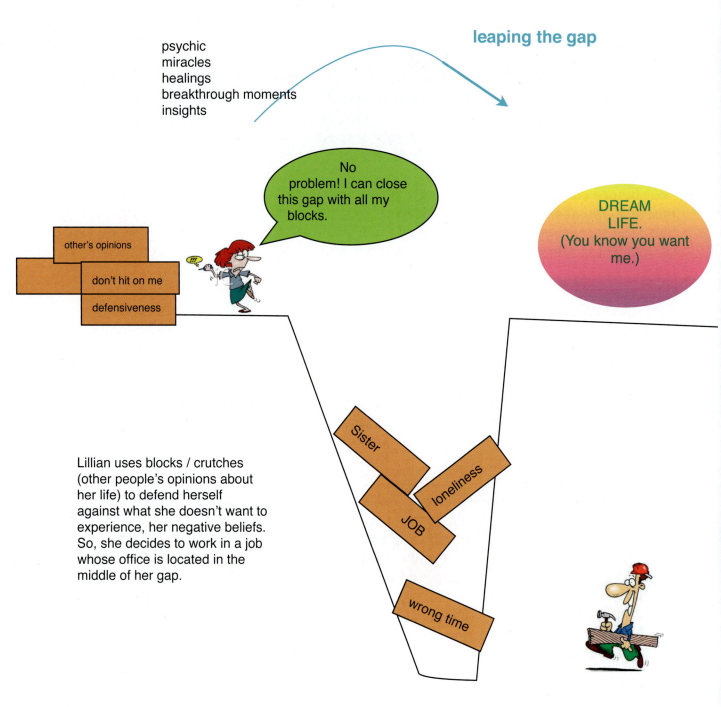

Ninth Session:
Money With Strings Attached
"Revenge Fat"

After Lake Tahoe, Lillian wanted to talk about her sister. The attacks were escalating just as we had predicted and her sister was now bad-mouthing Lillian to their parents.

"Let's talk about my sister," said Lillian.

"I know that my sister was bad mouthing me about being independent. I already knew it was coming," said Lillian to her mother.

Lillian's mom started to dog on Lillian, as well, acting as a mouthpiece for Ursela. She started to spit little wads of fire at Lillian for Ursela's sake. Ursela was thrilled that Mama was going to help her do her dragon work in the house where Lillian lived with her parents.

So what could Lillian do? Lillian suggested, "The only thing I can do is to produce big money results so that they can see that my decision to separate from my sister, Patricia and the office--- was the best decision."

Basically, Lillian said that she wanted to "prove" to them--- her parents and Ursela, that she was capable. In her own words, "I want them to know that I know what I am doing. I'm also trying to show mom and dad that Ursela is wrong. And to stop listening to her. Then, my parents will be like, 'Ursela, she's making money. Leave her alone.'"

Here again, Lillian is trying to "show off" to her parents and "prove" to them that her decisions are worthwhile. She is also trying to use them as guard dogs to fend off another alpha female threat.

Notice the words that I highlighted above:

Step 1: Find Key Statements

1. Proving to others that I am capable.
2. Having my decisions respected.
3. Fending off another alpha female threat.

Step 2; What is the opposite of these 3 statements?

1. People knowing that I am capable.
2. I don't have to explain my decisions.
3. I am surrounded by those whom I feel special and loved by.

So what Lillian really wanted, were these last 3 statements: to feel capable, respected and loved. She didn't want the prior 3 that she originally stated which was: to prove her abilities, force others to respect her and fend off threats.

But what I said was this: that ==Lillian can have what she wants, but she is placing all these conditions onto receiving it.==

Step 3: Let's look at the conditions:

1. In order to feel capable, which conditions must be met? Lillian has to prove it. How? By making tons of money, moving out of her parent's house and being self-reliant.

2. In order to feel like her decisions are respected, which conditions must be met? Lillian has to "show off" her success to her parents by flaunting it somehow. When her parents balk at her, "Well, maybe you could learn form Ursela and see how she does it? I don't see how you could just disregard your sister--- she's *your* sister!" So, Lillian would have to point to her brand new c-class Mercedes and then they, would zip their lips.

3. In order to be surrounded only by those who love and make Lillian feel special, which conditions must be met? Lillian must fend off threats from other alpha females, like her sister. She has to hug her dad and sweetly sing, "Give me some sugar," then kiss him on the cheek, high-five him and remind him, "I really love how we communicate honestly and had such a good time camping last week!" She has to get her father on her side.

Step 4: Problem Shooting

Lillian would not allow herself to have what she wants. She made it conditional. She had to WORK for it. She didn't just inherently KNOW that the universe was willing and prepared to deliver it to her with NO STRINGS ATTACHED. But she put a few puppet strings on there, attached those strings to her father, her mother and her sister.
And then the universe got all confused because should it have sent her some puppet money with puppet strings attached to these sort of pitiful looking puppets called her mom and her sister? Didn't she want some better looking, more sexy puppets, at least? Not the same old puppets that she's had for 18 years. Not the same damn puppets that were attached to all her fat.

The universe was thinking, "Damn. Didn't we just give her a fat abortion? What are all these strings attached to her money that are fatty strings? Is that girl still trying to heal her family? Oh no, we are not going to go through that again." So what did the universe do? Did it send Lillian some fatty greasy money? Or does it COCK-BLOCK her success?

Because the universe would rather Lillian be poor, skinny, sexy, good-looking, confident and happy in a romantic relationship AND a Lapis, then a miserable unromantic rich Blue Diamond like her sister.

Step 5: Having a conversation with the Universe:

Lillian said, "So are you saying that I am not accepting the money unless I am proving to my mom, dad and sister that I am capable? It has to be some big breakthrough--- it can't just be oh... I made some money."

"Let's have a conversation with the Universe. I will channel your spirit guides and Higher Self. You have a conversation with 'them' while I sit here," I said. Lillian agreed.

The Universe said, "You are saying to us, 'Give me some of that green stuff that you call cash.' We answer you by saying, sure, here you go babes. Whoa.. wait a second, now. Sweetheart, what are you going to do with this green stuff? You gonna smoke it or something?"

Lillian said, "No. I am going to use stacks of it to beat my family over the head. Then, I am going to rub some of it in Crisco and smear it on my sister's car. That way, they will respect my power."

The Universe said, "We would prefer for you to smoke it."

Lillian went, "Oh no. No no no. You see, I've been waiting 18 years to get revenge on everyone who ever told me I was fat, unlovable, incapable, stupid, sheep and who treated me like I didn't deserve anything. When I finally get some money--- I always promised myself that I was going to have, use and show off my beauty and never be ashamed of myself again!"

The universe said, "We believe in all of those things. But it's like we give you money and just like Jesus turned water into wine---- Lillian, you are going to turn money into revenge fat."

The Universe continued, "The hell we are! We just orchestrated 6 weeks of vision board counseling, 5 raunchy sobbing phone calls, we gave you Alan, we kicked you out of your office, we threatened to evict you from your home, we literally killed your sisterly relationship with Ursela, we beat you down with Dr. Susan's phone calls, we gave you a fat abortion, we stuck you in Lapis Land for 8 months--- we did not go through all that trouble, so that you could resurrect your fat via this new kind of fat called revenge fat. We just got rid of sad fat, angry fat, unworthy fat, sheep fat, ugly fat, karmic fat, genetic fat, little girl fat---- and now you come up with a new brand of fat that you wanna try out called revenge fat? Gurl! You are not fat. You will never be fat again. If you try to re-attach that fat to your midriff, we are going to have a hissy fit and we will dull your scissors. We will block you and you will never ever be able to get fat again. Your metabolism has changed permanently. Even surgery cannot help you get fat now. AND don't try to trick us. Who do you think we are? You cannot turn money into revenge fat. We won't let you. We let Jesus turn water into wine because his intentions were coming from joy. Your intentions to turn money into fat are coming from revenge. We won't agree."

"So explain to me exactly how I would get fat by getting money?" said Lillian. "You said that the money will only create more of those emotions between me and the family and potentially I will want to heal them again?"

I stopped channeling for a moment and started to have a conversation with Lillian as myself. Meaning, I started to talk to her in my own voice. The Universe or your Higher Self, similar to when you are having a conversation with an entity you refer to as, "God," speaks to you in a tone of voice similar to your own. God or even your own spirit guides will "match" your vibration, pound for pound. Meaning, if you have a southern accent and you use the words, "peach pie," a lot--- guess what? When you pray or receive Divine Guidance, God is going to speak in a southern accent. He/She is the master of communicating to even an enemy in his own voice.

Is your money spent and then, gone? Is it pearls thrown to swine?

Or is it a seed you plant in fertile soil? Does one seed grow for you a entire money garden?

I personally don't do that (most of the time). I talk like me, Olivia Lee. I am sensitive and when I feel or experience injustice, I become angry. I am not nearly as funny or compassionate as "the Universe." That is how I know when I am channeling a "higher force" or when I am not channeling and being myself. People ask, "This is sort of an amorphous line, no?" Yes. It's like being an actor. Some actors are well-trained Julliard level performers and can efficiently and cleanly separate their own personal lives from those of the characters they play on stage. Some cannot.

Okay, moving forward. So here I was, as myself, talking to Lillian. I also noticed that when I was channeling the "Universe" on Lillian's behalf, they were a bit "sassy." There was a lot of flare and a down-home goodness, a syrupy love.

Step 6: Re-working your intentions

Lillian asked, "How does receiving money at this point in my life, turn into fat?"

I put my 2 cents in, "It doesn't turn into fat. YOU turn it into fat with your intentions. Let's re-work your intentions. For example, if you get that Mercedes c-class, don't start rubbing your beautiful ass all over it in front of Ursela's driveway. Just drive it. Or, put some Wrapping In Love Technique into teaching others how to succeed, just as you did. So if you change your intentions, the Universe might change its mind. Remember, you are talking to the Golden Money Chute in the Sky.

"Right now, I feel like your intentions to get money is to build revenge fat. So, can we change that intention? How are you going to use the money that you earn now?"

When Lillian buys clothes with the intention of making her sister jealous, the money used to buy clothes makes her fat with revenge fat.

When Lillian buys clothes with the intention of paying back her father and feeling worthy enough to buy herself some new clothes, then the money she used to buy clothes sends forth love into the world---- and it brings back more money to her. Why? Because money with the intention of self-love is the same equation as money = self worth. Self worth, according to Lillian's Wrapping in Love Technique is a big income bringer.

==The same exact money and the same exact clothes will either bring Lillian jealousy and fat. OR love and more income.==

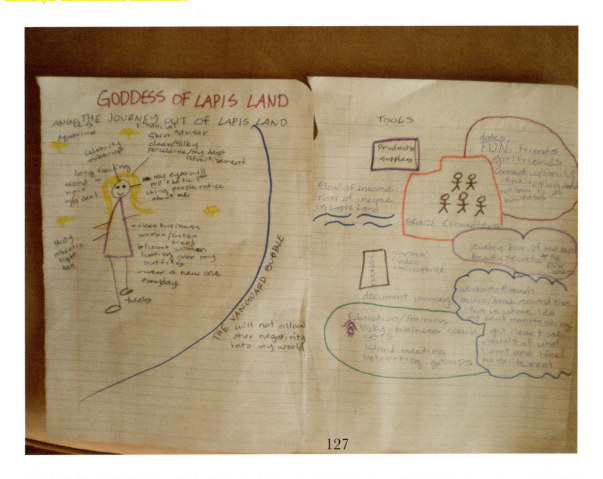

MONEY INTENTION CHART

How I earn money:	What I WANT to do with it:	How I change my intentions to incorporate my Higher Good:
Money is a step forward in my growth	Money is used once and disappears. Must earn more. Money = revenge fat	Money begets more money. Money = love
When I make Ruby Duby	Buy a Mercedes C-class and then drive it in a bikini to my sister's house to show off. wasting gas	Inspire my downline. Fill it with products to take to meetings. My company car. My car is my investment. Every mile I use it for, brings me more income.
When I get a big commission check	Buy new clothes. Be dressed to the top at every Saturday meeting to make my sister jealous and lose her breath. playing my sister's deadly game on her level. Ursela is not WORTH the money I spent on these clothes. I am! Money = clothes = jealousy = fat	Pay my dad back all the money I borrowed. I am worth the price of my new clothes. I am worth the debt that I pay back. My new clothes are a reflection of my new self. Everything I touch I would shine light on. Money is my love and LIGHT energy, that spreads through my garments out into the world.
moving out of my parent's house	Have a party. Invite Alan, my boyfriend over, decorate it with expensive furniture, romance and love, freedom! I try to pay rent each month, but stress over the lost income.	Create a working office space in my new place where I can have business meetings and women can come and heal. My apartment is my money garden. I grow prosperity, healing and community from this place.

Tenth Session:
Psychic Attacks

There are 2 "best" sources of information about psychic attacks. They are Sylvia Browne's books. She is a famous psychic. And then, there is the Devil (i.e. Satan). By the Devil, I mean something like a Satanic church, cult or violent drug ring--- any institution, formal or casual, where they can teach you how to exact your revenge in ritualistic detail. You can refer to either one of these sources and they can tell you a great deal.

In my opinion though, psychic attacks are really rare amoung gray souls. Gray souls are those who have not yet chosen to live as "light" beings here on planet Earth. They are sort of the "in-betweens." They aren't dark souls like serial killers, but they aren't saintly, either. The majority of people who live in the first world and are relatively middle to upper class, are primarily gray souls. I don't want to sound classist, but in my opinion, there are 2 systems that exist on planet Earth.

There is a system of success (corporate culture, electoral politics and Hollywood are examples) designed to kill you.

Then, there is a system of humanity designed to uplift you.

One promises success, wealth and vanity. It provides longevity on the physical material plane. It services your ego. The other is risky, has no guarantees, it allows you love and community--- but your life is not cushioned or supported ethically or otherwise, in order to survive. So we make our choices as souls. are we going to be gray or light?

Psychic attacks only happen to gray souls trying to turn light. Or to light souls just for being a light soul. If you are a light soul, you will be attacked. Unless you hide. Do you ever wonder why authors are notoriously reclusive? Think of J.D. Salinger. He lives in a log cabin in the woods and won't talk to anyone. It's been half a decade since he's emerged, publicly. So yes, a lot of souls go into hiding. Think of Native Americans. They don't share their cultural or sacred knowledge with the "white man." There is a respect and a deep level of protection on the part of light souls to keep what is holy to them and their people, holy. I'll give you another example: the Virgin Mary. What was she hiding? Jesus.

Even God hides, okay? This is a dark plane. Earth is one of the most negative planets in the galaxy. And we come here to experience darkness. Why? In order to expand our light. Why would we choose to be a light soul and then risk being pyschically attacked by either dark forces or dark souls? In order to expand our light. A secondary reason is to help uplift others.

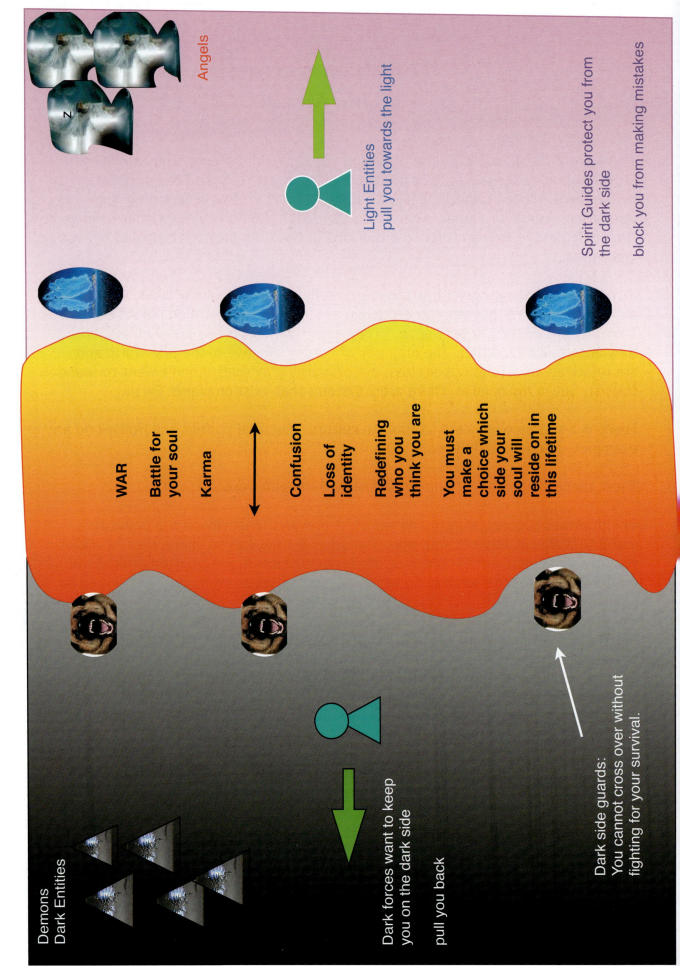

Preliminary guides for asking the Universe for answers:

Lillian had a bunch of questions about psychic attacks because she recently experienced one. Before we began, I wanted to know if she had anyone specific in mind whom she wanted me to channel: the Universe, Father God, Mother God, Jesus, Tina Turner? Because believe it or not, each of these entities would have a slightly different answer or perspective. For example, any time you ask Jesus a question, there's this damn "love your neighbor" blanket philosophy behind everything. Sometimes, I'd rather ask Tina Turner. Why does Jesus do this? Think about his role in the Universe--- the dude "rises above" sort of like Martin Luther King Jr.. Well, what if I don't want to rise above? What if I'm not ready for that? What if I want to kick ass and get a divorce? If I want to ask Jesus about a divorce, I better be VERY specific to him that I also intend to kick ass. Because his first answer is always going to be the most highest evolved answer that any human can achieve. If I were Ghandi or the Dalai Lama, I'd have no problem taking his advice. But if I am just plain old me, then I'll take what he said and twist it around to fit my needs.

ASKING THE RIGHT QUESTION TO THE RIGHT ENTITY is key. It's not that they don't give you the right answers. It's that we cannot hear them, truthfully. They can only speak to us on OUR level. As much as we can handle, bear to hear or take. They can't help us any more than we are willing or able to receive.

What can you receive? What are you willing to receive? How open of a channel will you allow yourself to be IN ORDER TO CHANGE?

Step 1: Who do you want to ask?

When I asked Lillian who she wanted me to channel, she said, "the Universe." I had to ask her who this consists of. Could she be specific, as well as saying the Universe?

"I always think of my spirit guides and all the angels," she said.

"Which kind of angels? There are archangel,s the big wigs who talk to Father and Mother God in council, there are personal angels and guardian ones?" I asked.

"Guardian angels," she said.

"How many?" I asked.

"Three?"

"Okay, who else? Like your Higher Self?"

"I think the guardian angels because they are the ones that absorbed 80% of the attack and they kind of know who it is coming from," she said.

"Yes, you are right. They have a bird eye's view of things. Unfortunately, angels are mute. They don't talk. So I would have to do some sign language. Can you pick someone who chats a lot? Like I dunno…"

"This whole world is all new to me. I wasn't aware of the structure of all this," said Lillian. "What about just asking my spirit guides?"

"Good, let's include them. But they have limited knowledge because they are blocked from seeing certain attacks, just as you are. It is in their karmic agreement to go through life WITH you and they are learning, as well. I get most of my gossip about you from them, anyways," I said.

"We should pick Mother God, I think. She's a good one. Very wise. But we need an expert on psychic attack. I think Jesus is okay. He can put his 2 cents in, we don't have to listen to EVERYTHING he says. But I'm sure he's got awesome advice," I said.

> *A psychic attack is when a dark or gray spirit is sending you conscious and deliberate negative attention.*
>
> *Only people who have gray souls can psychically attack anyone.*
>
> *If you are a light being, your only power to hurt someone is your forgiveness of their soul.*

I stopped for a minute, closed my eyes and meditated. Usually, I can get a sense of who is in the room with us. Sometimes, a dead grandmother shows up. You never know. But the key is to ask for spiritual help. Then, see who arrives to aide you. It's very specific to your specific needs, in the moment. If Lillian were trying to win Wimbleton, probably some tennis playing spirit guides would show up. But in this case, she is asking about her recent psychic attack.

The spirit world knows exactly where you are at, what you need and what you are seeking. They are specific. Usually, we are not. We don't take these details seriously enough. We think that "help" is "help." We are very general about what we ask for. So, we get general answers like, "Do unto your neighbor…" We need to be specific not only about our questions, but about who we want help from.

The universe is a resource. We have to learn how to use it to our advantage.

Step 2: Say a prayer and call in your spirit guides

You can use any prayer you wish, but it's nice to make up your own prayer.

Lillian felt like all this junk inside her body is blocked from coming out. She had a runny nose, congestion, constipation, nausea. Then, she went into my bathroom and vomitted. She came out feeling better.

Declare who you are in the name of a higher power.

"What do you call yourself when you are a celebrity/philathropist, meaning when you are in your full power," I asked.

"I am Leader Teacher Lillian, in the name of Mother Nature."

Tell me your purpose:

"To give women their life and power, back."

"Back from where? Where it has been lost to?"

"From the prison of being overweight."

That was sort of the crux of our prayer. We were going to make the second half of the prayer a "rebuke" or a conquering of the demon or dark force that wanted to keep these women inside their own prison.

We had to name the demon. In church, it's Satan. But in this case, it was the workers of a Dark Force called Fat, which were Lillian's healing agreements. So one of Lillian's P.O.W.'s was resenting leaving the prison.

"They want you to construct more blubber walls, for them," I said. "So you not only have to set your prisoner free from your fat. You must do it with love. So part of your declaration statement to the devil of Fat is a statement of healing and freedom to your former prisoner. How are you going to rebuke this demon who is torturing you?"

Lillian thought that her primary attacker was Ursela. So she had to think of a way to rebuke Ursela, in the name of Mother Nature. She was stumped.

"Let's think of your greatest power and strength as a leader/teacher," I said. "Love is the over-arching philosophy. But it isn't a tool. **Tools are strategies, processes or lessons which helped you free yourself** from the prison of fat."

Lillian said, "Saying 'no' is a huge strategy."

"What else helped you get through the fat period?" I asked.

"To always carry myself as though the Golden Money Chute in the Sky was watching."

"So, the Universe as my witness, I walk forward with..."

"Certainty," she said.

"What else?"

"Confidence, poise and grace."

"I'm just gonna be honest with you, poise and grace aren't going to rebuke the demon of fat---"

"Wait----" she interuppted me, "faith, courage."

"So here we have it----

"I am Leader Teacher Lillian, in the name of Mother Nature. I teach women how to get their life and power back from the prison of being overweight. With the Universe as my witness, I walk forward with certainty, faith and courage. When the fat rises to attack me...

"Give me your biggest threat. Meaning, I want you to threaten this fat to step back or else it's going to get shot. You've got a lot of spirit guides on your side and you are warning that fat, don't come near me because I am going to be just fine. You on the other hand, are going to fry. So tell me what your flame is made of?"

==Rebuke your enemy.==

"It's my jovial aura," said Lillian.

"How does it burn it?"

"It fries it," she answered.

"What is the result of frying fat?" I asked.

"Can't attack me afterwards," she said. "It's fried. OR... another way is to use a mirror, so that the fat is fried by looking at its own reflection in the mirror. It is battling itself and not battling me."

"So, your jovial aura works like a mirror," I said. "The fat is fried by looking at its own reflection and begins to battle itself. Meanwhile, I take my memories and lessons which I have learned from battling fat in the past--- and I use the corpse of the demon called FAT, and a package it up as fried pork skins and sell this to millions of women and call it 'My Victory' brand weight-loss chips. A subsidary of Wrapping in Love Corporation."

==Forgive your enemy with your core positive belief.== Our final prayer was:

"I am Leader Teacher Lillian, in the name of Mother Nature. I teach women how to get their life and power back from the prison of being overweight. With the Universe as my witness, I walk forward with certainty, faith and courage. When the fat rises to attack me, my jovial aura is a mirror that fries fat with its own reflection. Fat melting feels like love. I forgive my fat and release it in the name of Wrapping in Love Technique."

Step 3: Figure out who is attacking you

Lillian had a bunch of questions on this subject. I channeled her spirit guides for the entire session, so the following does not represent my personal views. It is the opinion of a couple of her spirit guides who are speaking to her particular situation.

Lillian: "Is this psychic attack a joint effort between Dr. Susan and Ursela?"

Spirit Guides: Yes.

Lillian: Are my symptoms a result of a psychic attack or should I own them as my own self-created fear?

Spirit Guides: Do not own them as your own.

Lillian: How conscious is Ursela of this psychic attack? I get she is stepping up to her role in my Ike and Tina Turner drama, but is she on a conscious level out to destroy me?

Spirit Guides: Yes.

Lillian: Did she really plan to make me physically ill on a conscious level or did she just plan to turn my family and friends against me which led to all the physical ailments?

Spirit Guides: Both.

Lillian: How do I prevent further psychic attacks as my future success will threaten her even more?

Spirit Guides: You can't. They get bigger and bigger. But you know what? You grow greater and greater and what seems BIG to them as far as a psychic attack goes---to you, soon, will feel like another challenge. Another monster to slay so that you get to be lauded as a hero. Another hardship so that you get to identify with more women in America and become a celebrity/philanthropist.

In essense, each pyschic attack is a "degree" like a master's degree, a certificate, an award signifying graduation. It's just more stuff to put on your Oprah resume. Each psychic attack will earn you a degree in Wrapping In Love University. You know how you have Team Elite University at your company? In the empire of Lillian, you will have your own university and training ground for facilitators of your "sensitive overweight women" groups. There will be specialities such as domestic abuse, poverty, self-love, etc.---- but you have to be a master or teacher of each field. Just a smattering of each understanding.

What you don't know now, get ready. You are about to learn it. If you don't learn it before you become celebrity/philanthropist, you will learn it WHILE you are celebrity/philanthropist. How do you think Oprah felt losing 60 pounds on national television... and then gaining it all back... on national television? What you don't get now, you will learn later. Be thankful no one is watching you right now when you have the luxury of being a mess. Later on, there will be millions.

Lillian: Is Ursela really clueless about why I want nothing to do with her?

Spirit Guides: Not really.

Lillian: I'm having all of these symptoms of a classic psychic attack? Have I created this or is this my psychic attacker?

> *You know that you are being psychically attacked if you have just taken a big step in your spiritual growth and then you immediately get sick.*

Vicky: I think it's your sister. I don't think that these are your natural feelings of anxiety. I think that they are artifically induced by an outside force.

Spirit Guides: The goal of a psychic attacker is to convince you that you are not who you think you are. What you think of as "money" or any form of power is not actually of benefit to you. It has "conditions." Meaning, a psychic attacker will subtly demonstrate to you or teach you (hopefully they have gotten you under their wing) and try to ingrain the message into you that what you want--- let's say, it's money. That money can be had, but ONLY under certain restricted conditions. And they are going to doctor or mentor or help you get through the bureaucracy of those conditions. In other words, they are the secret key to your power. Without them, you can never access who you truly are.

They are a sort of glorified middle man, a manager or a publicist. They are the buffer, in-between, man behind the curtain, the invisible hidden weapon or force that fuels all of your important decisions. They are the puppeteer who is not seen by the audience, but remains off-stage. Why do they not take center stage? If they are so powerful, then why do they need to reap your rewards? Why do they need to get power or money through you? Why don't they just go out and make their own money if they are the so-called knower of all the secrets to power? Why do they so adamanetly need you?

Because they don't want to be seen. They don't want the limelight. They want to stay in the background. Because they are criminals and they know that as soon as your family or good friends find out that they are the ones who are secretly manipulating you, people are going to start to tell you the truth about them--- that they are con-men and are tricking you. So they go through a lot of trouble to remain hidden. To "pass on the leadership" so that they don't get blamed.

Ironically, as egotistical as they are, they don't like to be "star." They like to be the star's romantic partner or spouse. They also like to be the vice-president instead of the president, or the president's secret advisor. But they are always underground and not on-stage. They don't like to be photographed. They don't like to get public attention. Why? Because they know deep down inside, that one day people are going to figure out this scam. And they don't want to be the target of all that negative attention. In other words, they don't want to be the one who takes the bullet. They want to set you up as the hero... who will one day take the fall. But they get to run away if they are invisible and in the background, with all your money and treasures.

Psychic attackers are the most patient people in the whole world. They will groom a potential victim for years. Think of a child molester who will gain the trust of a child for months or years before molesting. They do not want to get caught. If the child at any point, decides to rebel against the molester, the molester will cut him loose. It's not worth the risk. So psychic attackers will groom several potential victims at the same time and one day, one of those victims which shows a lot of promise will mature and then, be ripe for taking advantage of. So in the "grooming" process, there isn't a lot of stake for the attacker. But once that victim matures, the psychic attacker will probably never let that victim go.

A pyschic attack can feel like anything from a common cold, to a rash covering your whole body or anxiety and depression.

Why? Think again of the child molester. Once he has molested a child, do you think he will let that kid run off and start becoming a chatty teenager who talks about all his dark memories when he gets drunk? Oh no. The molester has to control this child for the rest of his life, so that the molester never gets caught.

Once you are intimate with a pyschic attacker, they "own" you. They consider everything that you do, as a potential risk to them---- either getting caught or affecting their personal well-being.

Once you have a relationship with a psychic attacker, you are forever their liability. At this point, I suggest prayer because it helps to have spiritual protection. Because whatever you do on the physical plane, besides running away where they can't find you---- they project this oppressive aura onto you and those around you. They target you with what I call "threat."

Prior to trying to break away from a psychic attacker, you will be treated like a god. You will be spoiled, groomed, taught the insider secrets to success. You are favored and hooked up with important people who will also teach you how to climb the ladder of power and success. You are given a backstage pass to all the best shows, you meet the best artists, the best performers and their management teams---- basically, you meet all the universally accepted "celebrities" of stardom. Basically, the psychic attacker will introduce you to other "victims" who have succeeded with their own personal psychic attackers standing right by their side. And they want to show you, "See? You could be just like them?"

Conformity is KEY. Psychic attackers need you to be pliable enough to "succeed" in their eyes. They need you to conform to their system of thought, their model of the world, their idea of success, their way of sneaking around the rules that apply to almost everyone else.

If you ever go against the grain or don't follow his/her system to the "t," then he will call you or others who agree with you, as "disappointments." Even if you point out how those people managed to succeed through a system that is different from his--- he will find a reason, regardless of how far-fetched, why those people are dangerous. He especially hates those who make it "on their own" without a personal psychic attacker by their side. If you speak or cavort with those kinds of people, you will be punished. For this is one of his greatest threats. That you would find out the truth and turn it on him.

The goal of every psychic attacker is to find victims who will reap more victims for him/her. The best victim is one who goes out and finds more victims. That way the psychic attacker can feed his/her own addiction to power, through both quality of victims and quantity. The goal of most psychic attackers is to expand their territory or reach. They want to have great influence, even as an underground or invisible force.

Unfortunately, most of them cannot experience joy. So they get bored easily, even while they are patiently grooming more victims. Ironically, the more they attack---- the less satisfied they are with the scale of those attacks. It's like a sexual abuser who needs you to scream for him or at least feign like you are in pain. They get off on it. So if the attacker isn't amusing himself enough with his success and feels slightly unworthy---- then he is going to look outwards and definitely blame you for that unsatisfied appetite.

The progession of every psychic attacker is to look for bigger fish. Meaning, one day he is going to pick a "quality victim" who turns out to be a psychic attacker, herself. And then the fire-spitting is going to escalate into a type of war. Smart psychic attackers, who at their core are living their lives through fear will recognize this and RUN! The cocky psychic attacker will try to treat the other psychic attacker just like a victim. And that is obviously not going to work out.

ALMOST EVERY single psychic attacker you meet, will underneath the surface of their personality know how to at least act or be humble. Because once they cross the line of danger, they will be destroyed. They have studied and carefully watched other psychic attackers fall from the demon's grace by being too arrogant to sense when they are going to get caught.

When you are in despair, when you are in grief or hopelessness, any type of anxiety---- your psychic attacker is going to be overjoyed. In fact, this is the only way that he can feel joy. Psychic attackers can only feel joy or beauty or appreciation for another's soul in the midst of destroying that soul. I have just described a murderer. But most psychic attackers don't murder on a physical level. They prefer to drain you of your life force over a period of many years, such as a life time.
Because they cannot live without you. You are like a battery or a source of energy for them. Attackers rely on victims to survive on a daily basis.

You can't really end a relationship with a psychic attacker. It's so internal. But you can release them. You can severe your karmic agreement with them. You can also go on living without thinking about them or living as though they don't exist. Simply put, you just move on.

The fear is that all your scars of abuse or all that anxiety and fear that they instilled into you is going to resurface one day. Or you are going to meet another wonderful man who will one day cheat on you and how are you going to deal with that when the time comes? You think of revenge tactics or pre-nups or whatever bandaide gets you through. But the reality is, you are probably not going to meet another psychic attacker. Unless you really want one.

> *Lillian woke up in Lake Tahoe with a sore throat, bad cough and fever.*
>
> *Her sister had sent her a psychic attack.*

Psychic attackers sense when victims have overcome and won't return back to that dark abyss. Usually, *they* are not attracted to *you*, anymore.

So your fears of every getting involved with another psychic attacker are most likely, unfounded. It's all in your head. So my advice is just move on. You'll never see them again. You'll never hear from them again. Once they realize that you have set them loose, they just disappear and give up. Unlike love, they never hold on to the hope of seeing you again, one day. They simply don't care anymore.

Step 4: Release them or place them in the hands of the Holy Spirit

It is now out of your hands. Once you release your psyhic attackers, Jesus, Mother God and your spirit guides--- whoever you called in to help release you from your pain will take over. Your attackers are sent out into the ethers and are now the responsibility of the Universe.

While Lillian was chanting her prayer outloud, I smoked an herbal blend of sage, rosemary, lavendar and dried rose petals. I imagined it not going into my lungs, but into my bone marrow, purifying it. As she spoke her prayer, she began to cough. This was her grief energy in her chest trying to keep her from saying her prayer. Because with every word she spoke affirming her higher soul purpose--- the pyschic attacker was losing hold on her body, unable to weaken her from living her life free from pain and grief. I also put on some gospel music in the background to help me to focus.

Lillian: In regards to my business, I have constant anxiety and dread and I read these are symptoms of a psychic attack. Is this a major reason why I feel so stuck, blank, and fearful in my business?

Spirit Guides: There are 2 purposes for you to feel anxiety. Your spirit guides have the most clearest ability to send you messages right when you wake up. Because you are fresh and open to receiving their communication after a long out-of-body sleep. Why? Because your brain is relatively empty of thoughts. In other words, you have no resistance right when you wake up. They are making you feel anxious because they are warning you about your psychic attacker. As the day moves forward, the anxiety lessons because you are able to rationalize away why working with your sister is an okay idea. You sort of are able to use the power of your mind to overcome your anxiety and in a sense, erase the warnings of your spirit guides. You ignore or override your intuition with your brain.

Lillian: No wonder, the office makes me sick when I think about walking into that place.

Spirit Guides: Your spirit guides are saying, "Are you going to go back to work with that psychic attacker?" So they are sending you a "red flag." Now, they are quite aware that you don't know what this red flag means. But they do know that you can easily sense and feel EMOTION. So they primarily use your emotions in order to communicate with you.

The second purpose of waking up with anxiety is this: What is fear? What is anxiety? What is powerlessness? It is a lack of faith in yourself. To a certain extent, it is a lack of faith in the universe who has vowed to protect you and respond to your every prayer. But what is it really?

It is power. It is a mirror of all your power. You can only see the darkness when light is present. You have no awareness of how pitch black things are until you experience contrast such a single flickering candle in the midst of a storm. You have no awareness of light until you put a speck of darkness in there--- such as lock yourself in a closet for 5 years and then walk out into the blaring sunlight. It will blind you.

Do you know the feeling at the top of a roller coaster? Do you know the feeling of a man who has been paralyzed for his whole life and taken the first step? You see when a psychic attacker pushes you to the ends of your rope, strangles the life out of you and when you begin to realize that for the first time in your WHOLE LIFE you are going to take your first breath without his hands around your throat---- all those doubts and feelings and thoughts and memories are going to rise up the surface... in order to be released.

It's like a line of prisoners lining up at the gate of freedom. Like the Jewish concentration camp prisoners waiting at the gate for the American soldiers to unlock that gate because the Nazi regime has been defeated. All your thoughts of self-doubt have surfaced, lined up at the gate of freedom....

And the anxiety that you are feeling are all your spirit guides.... waiting for you to take that first breath of freedom. They are over-excited at your new journey. But all you can think of... is what you are leaving behind.

It's like the concentration camp prisoners, looking back at all that they have suffered and remembering all those years of pain and now that they are finally leaving their prison, they can't feel joy or happiness. They only feel grief and pain and heartache for all the casualties. For years, they held those feelings inside of themselves to keep from crying and then getting shot by the guards. And finally, all those feelings are being set free and allowed to surface. One last blow, before they are at last... relinquished forever.

The sales style that Lillian was taught by her upline was called, "Bait and Hook."

The key is to have those feelings, listen to the higher message blaring above your pain, "The Nazi's have been defeated. You are free to go!" And then allow the grace of God to fall upon you like going over the edge of a giant rollercoaster.

This pain, this elation, this strong undeniable anxiety and horrific fear--- it is the precursor to a stronger, more powerful force that exists within you called forgiveness.

Lillian: The only part I'm confused about is the prisoners lining up at the gate--- I've already experienced that, right?

Spirit Guides: Yes, every morning when you woke up with anxiety--- those were your feelings of self-doubt lining up, ready to be released. But instead of feeling your emotions and listening to the Higher Power that was sending you a message through your own emotions---- you rationalized that feeling and went to work, anyways. You sort of ignored the message.

==Think of your negative emotions as mail from God. You got the mail. But you didn't open it and read it.==

Lillian: I can tell you why I didn't open up the mail. I told myself that it was my fault I was feeling this way, that I'm just being silly. And it was something that I needed to overcome.

Spirit Guides: That is your psychic attacker, your sister as your perfect pimp shepherd--- training you WELL. You acted like her perfectly well-trained sheep, having feelings and thoughts that OVERRIDED your own emotional guidance and the messages of your own spirit guides.

Lillian: Why is it said that a psychic attack is evidence that good is rising beyond?

Spirit Guides: Because the dark side would have no reason to attack you unless you were trying to move forward. Good obedient prisoners are not disciplined. Powerful, rebellious, smart and those with undying faith in their own abilities to defeat their oppressors are punished, killed and beat down.

> *Lillian's natural sales style was called, "Wrapping in Love Technique."*

If they are coming after you, it is for a reason. You know the way out. You have the key to freedom and are not afraid to use it.

Lillian: Now that I know that, is there going to be a big release for the leftover feelings of self-doubt that I still experience?

Spirit Guides: This is why you are sick. You are releasing the leftover psychic attack. Often, when someone gets psychically attacked--- they also get sick. It is extremely common, in fact almost unavoidable. You are physical beings. Your spiritual body is intimately connected with your human body and your emotional body-- in fact, if you are able to harness the connection of your spiritual and physical--- you will become like Jesus. You will be able to heal broken bones and leprosy by touching someone with your hand.

But on a lower level, you manifest illness such as your sore throat and cough--- and that is your version of "going over the giant fall of the rollercoaster." It helps you to know that you are done with your prison. You are sick, you know why? Not because you were in a prison for so long and the prison made you sick. But because you just took your first breath of fresh clean air and your prisoner lungs aren't used to air that is not infested and dirty. You are feeling health, more than you are feeling any psychic attack.

The illness is showing you not that you are ill TODAY with your sore throat. The illness is showing you that, "Look how you have allowed yourself to live for 9 months working with your sister. Look at how you have lived in your prison with no fresh air." With the first breath of clean air---- NOW YOU KNOW what it feels like to be free! The air is so frickin clean that IT HURTS.

When darkness is pierced by a single ray of light--- darkness shatters. Is it the darkness you are feeling? Or the light?

When ego is touched by a moment of true love--- ego begins to die. Is it ego that is suffering from its own arrogance? Or is it love breaking its heart? It is love.

The only thing that is powerful enough to hurt and pain your powerful soul, my friend, is LOVE. You are feeling love, not pain. You are feeling light, not darkness. You are feeling your empowerment, not your past wounds. You are feeling your freedom and not your prison. This is you, who you are and it brings you pain to realize and see how much you have allowed yourself to hide behind your fat and your agreeements to heal others. You are feeling the power of your own soul roaring to get out of your heart and make money in the world, to uplift souls, to become a celebrity/philanthropist. You are feeling the PAIN of not allowing yourself to be WHO YOU REALLY ARE.

This is the only regret, the only pain. It is self-love.

Step 5: Receiving an answer

At that point, Lillian no longer needed me to channel her spirit guides for her. She just asked a question in her own mind and then automatically received an answer. Her focus was "how to make money" now that she had successfully released her fat and her healing agreement with her sister, who also played the role of her psychic attacker.

Lillian: How am I going to find my downline?

Spirit Guides: Everyone you are coming in contact with you senses your resistance. It is just like when you went fishing this past week with your father on this camping trip. The other fishermen told you that this was a protected lake, so they breed fish in there. There are so many minnows, that they won't bite if they feel even a little bit of resistance on the fishing line. So all these fish were biting, but none of them would commit.

Lillian: So how do I get past the fear?

Spirit Guides: You are hiding behind your fear or your fat. If you just let that go, then the "real" you can shine. And then all the minnows will find you. Just like that lady in the meeting who walked all the way from the back of the crowd to come talk to you. She was so excited about what you were selling and wanted to sign up right away.

Lillian: I just can see myself in my imagination as joyful, smiling and playing. I'm thinking to myself, "Man, I miss that girl." I'm having a vision right now of someone tapping me on the shoulder, coming out of nowhere. I turn around and even though we don't know each other, we are so excited to see each other. Immediately, I go into the teacher role and I know that she is someone that I have to work with.

So, how do I make money with her?

(Immediately, Lillian has another vision in her head in answer to her question. She recounts this vision to me.)

Lillian: Her and I were working together and there was never a struggle. It was just so natural. I knew exactly what to do, I was confident and the leader in the situation. She was so excited about the results coming in. Then, the money comes in. So, the relationship is built FIRST. The money follows.

==Once I switched into the mind-set that, "I am helping a soul, here. I knew exactly what to do. It was so natural."==

Shared victory. Noble. My money was bigger than hers, but I felt like it was well-deserved because I loved her through it. Money came in 10 fold to what was expected. It never felt it was like business, because the purpose was to uplift another soul. It became really contagious among the 2 of us.

PRAYER CARDS

Prayer cards are mantras or personalized positive "I" statements that you make either to yourself or the universe stating who you are, what you intentions are, what your higher purpose is and how you affect change in the world. They hold power because they are the truest affirmation of your soul path. When you say them outloud, you emanate a vibration that is uniquely YOU. Your prayer is WHO YOU ARE and you say it until the rest of you, comes into alignment with your highest self.

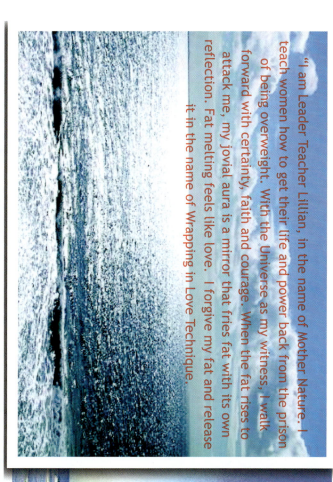

"I am Leader Teacher Lillian, in the name of Mother Nature. I teach women how to get their life and power back from the prison of being overweight. With the Universe as my witness, I walk forward with certainty, faith and courage. When the fat rises to attack me, my jovial aura is a mirror that fries fat with its own reflection. Fat melting feels like love. I forgive my fat and release it in the name of Wrapping in Love Technique."

Samples of prayer cards that Lillian and I printed out on an 8.5 X 11 page, then cut out. She placed them on her bathroom mirror, on her fridge, the dashboard of her car and in her purse.
Whenever she began to doubt herself, she would read the card and remind herself of who she is.

Eleventh Session:
The song of YES

Soon after Lillian's fat abortion and simultaneous psychic attack from her sister, she started receiving inspiration about how to expand her business. She would lie awake at night right before falling asleep and her spiritual dream team would send her visions of the meetings she was supposed to set up with Dr. Susan. Instead, Lillian would run those meetings by herself. She was to give herself the title, "The brains behind beauty."

Instead of the "bait and hook" routine that her sister had taught her, Lillian was now going to use her own personalized style of selling called, "Wrapping in Love Technique."

When I met with Lillian, she told her me vision. We started right away by drawing a picture of it.

"What does it look like?" I asked her.

"It's a beauty class and I'm the beauty teacher," she said.

"Where is it?" I asked.

"Our old meetings with Ursela were in her office. A sterile setting with desks. But I think I'd like my meetings to be in a day spa."

"Are there tables or chairs, pillows?" I asked.

Lillian thought about it. "There is one round table." She drew it on her paper.

"How many women are there?" I asked.

"Maybe, 9?" she said.

"Who are they?" I asked. Lillian looked confused. "Just make it up. We're going to do a mock beauty class, so you have to imagine your perfect customers. After all, part of your Wrapping in Love Technique is about merging their soul paths with financial gain. So, we need to know who these women are."

"Oh, okay," Lillian began listing the women as a personal trainer, plastic surgeon's wife, model in her 30's, a school teacher, president of a sorority, massage therapist, financial advisor, professional make-up artist and an ex Avon representative.

"What do they want, besides to look better? What are their souls looking for?" I asked.

"Um…" Lillian sat there, drawing a blank.

"Ask your spiritual dream team. Close your eyes, become quiet and ask the question into the ethers," I said.

"They want to see their inner beauty," she answered.

"Great. So now, let's talk about your presentation. This is a Wrapping in Love presentation, right?" I asked.

"Yes."

"So you have to be as integrous as possible. You have to be able to present to your customers varying and controversial perspectives of anti-aging and cite independent medical sources for each view point," I said. "You have to do an insane amount of extra research, similar to how a doctor or pharmacist would study or approach the subject of anti-aging."

"Okay," Lillian wrote that into her drawing.

We talked about all the supplies she would have on the table for her potential customers, the slide projector screen, the Zen-like sink area with a wicker basket of towels and the "store" area where the women could purchase her products on the spot. Lastly, we came up with an exercise using a hand-held mirror in which the women could bond emotionally with one another by focusing on their inner beauty.

The stickler for Lillian, was "research." She had always relied on Ursela or Dr. Susan to provide scientific details of how their products were manufactured, studied or offered proven results. When I approached Lillian about doing her own research, she hit up against a core negative belief of, "I'm not capable."

"This is so typical of me," she said, "I always rely on others to step in when I hit a road block. I don't believe that I can make it on my own."

"That's the brain-washing of your long-time pimp shepherd--- that you can't make it on your own. That's what Ike said to Tina Turner. That's the lie," I said. "You have to trust your dream team that you can do better and have more, on your own than as anyone else's sheep."

"How do I even go about doing this research?" she asked. "I've tried before by going to the research and development (R & D) department of our company. But so much of this information is hidden or top-secret. That's why I partnered with Dr. Susan. As an M.D., she was privy to the clinical studies. She got to enter into the lab's at our

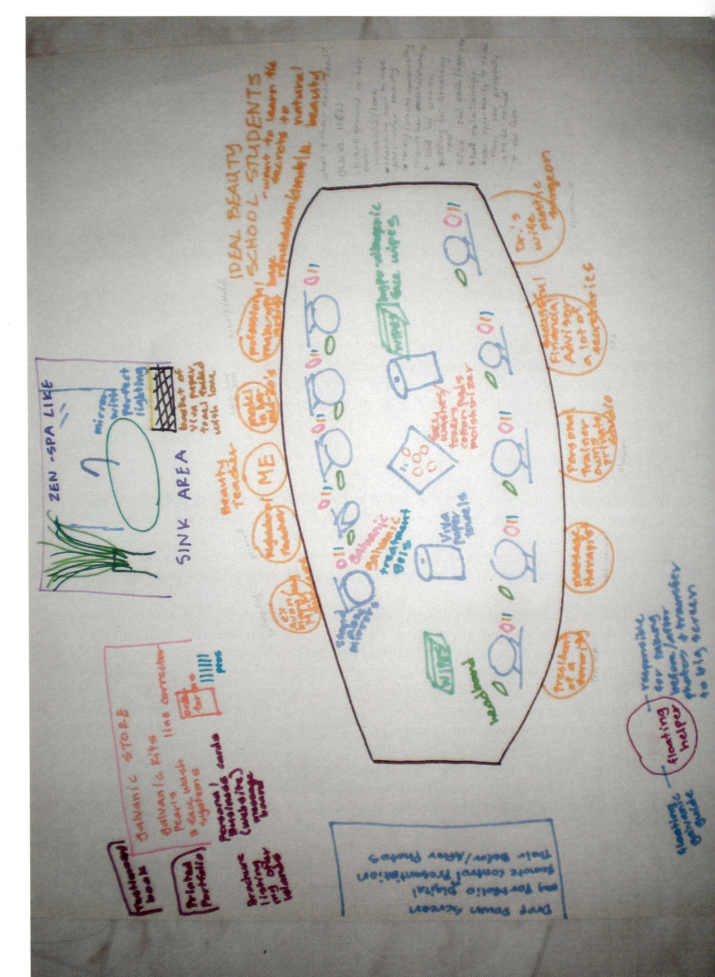

company and observe what they were doing. I feel so small, in comparison to her and Ursela. I can't even get past the front desk to take a look inside the lab, much less start asking the pharmaceutical engineers some research questions."

"You can do this!" I tried to snap her out of it. "What confuses you the most about this research?"

Lillian came up with a list:

- What questions do I ask about anti-aging?
- Who do I ask?
- How do I ask?
- What format will the answer come in?

"I want you to ask your spiritual dream team this list of questions," I said to her. She looked at me like a puppy dog. "But when you ask these questions, I want you to EXPECT an answer."

At this point, I channeled a bulleted list of "pointers" from her spirit guides. Regardless of whether Lillian was going to visit the library, a book store or the lab at her company--- she was going to find the answers to her research to help her build her new presentation based on Wrapping in Love. Before she even began, she started with a self-defeating attitude. To combat this, her dream team said:

The difference is: not knowing if the R & D department at my company is going to answer my questions, so I approach the woman at the front desk with the attitude of, "Let's see if she will help me."

OR

I already sat down and asked my higher self what questions I should ask the R & D department, who I should ask and what format the answers will come in. Although I don't know what the answers will be, I KNOW I WILL RECEIVE AN ANSWER.

If I ask someone and they block/reject me, I will look them in the eye and say, "I know what I am looking for. I know you can point me in the correct direction. Why would my higher self direct me here to you if I doubted myself?

Before I even ask, I have created an expectation that I will be answered. I do not create the expectation of, "Maybe they'll give me an answer? Maybe they won't have an answer? Maybe I don't know what I'm doing?"

I did my part. I stepped up. Now, the universe does its part and others step up to me to match my vibration.

I know what I want. I don't know how I am going to get it, but my higher self gives me the correct questions to ask and then sends me out into the world with this set of key questions. Armed only with this set of questions, I shout to the world and demand of them, "You will give me an answer! God, herself, has given me questions. God is also called my higher or inner self. I don't know what kind of answers you are going to give me, but if they are unsatisfactory, I am going to keep asking them." They better well give me some damn new different and more profound answers. They better keep feeding me new solutions until I am full.

My inner self did not give me a question that it did not expect to be answered. The higher I go, the more the doubt within me swells into my lungs like the ocean. The higher I am forced to fly, the harder, the longer, the more brilliant I must beat my wings against the wind of time and hope. I am a songbird of freedom, an intelligent instrument of prayer. I DO NOT ACCEPT THE ANSWER "NO" because I have not said 'no' to myself, yet. And if I have, I deeply regret my loss, but you know what? I swallow that along with my pride into the belly of my desire and it fuels the flame of what I call passion. From now on, I only say YES and the universe unerringly responds YES back to me, infinitely. It is a chorus, a choir, an orchestra, a symphony, a song, a mantra called YES.

"This is me." (DON'T EVER SAY "NO" TO ME, AGAIN)

After this monologue, Lillian suddenly received more inspiration on exactly what kind of research she needed to do. We wrote the inspired list down on her drawing.

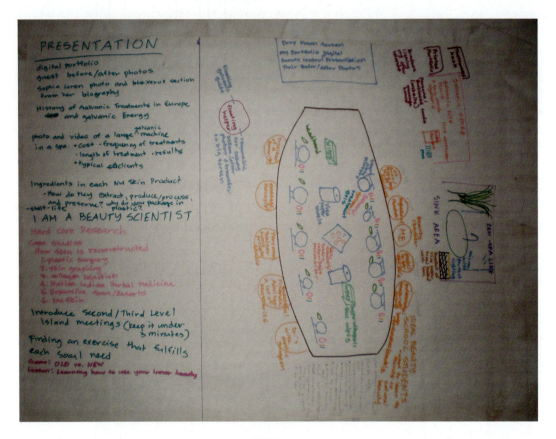

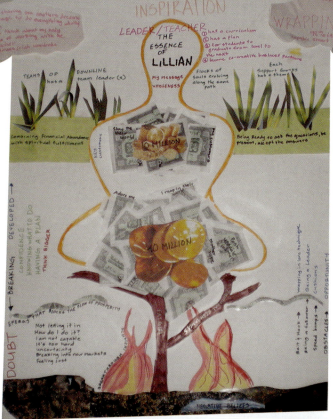

Aloha

Thank you for taking the time to read this book and share it with those whom you think may benefit from it.

In the future, I will hold classes for those wanting to learn how to build their vision boards, step by step. Please visit my website at www.visionboardworkbook.com for updates.

This is the first vision board guidebook in a series of 4 books. It was meant to introduce you to the basic foundational tools of how I help my clients discover and build their visions. The other guidebooks go into more depth. They will be published soon:

Vision Boards Workbook 1 Supplement: Cracking the Money/Doubt Code
follows up with what happens to Lillian after she teaches her first beauty class and begins to build her business with her personal sales style called, "Wrapping in Love Technique."

Vision Boards Workbook 2: Respect vs. Love, the Power of Anger
goes deeper into the mythology behind our soul paths. Its premise is that love is based on need and respect is based on choice. Often times, we will sacrifice one for the other. This workbook shows how a few powerful women have done that throughout their lives. The result is both hilarious and profound.

I was born in a stellium where 6 of my 12 planets were lumped together in the house of scorpio. Pluto, this evil star meteorite who makes its orbit around planet Earth once every 238 years, went over all 6 of those planets and blew my life to pieces each time it did. The result is that I have been forced to "transform" every other year since the age of 13.

I also have a feng shui number of 8, the Chinese symbol for infinity and power. It means that your bad is so very bad and your good, is beyond goodness. I have lived both in my lifetime. My karma is such that I am destined to use my psychic abilities to serve humankind. Nothing else will give me joy and the beauty that I long for. Every time I tried to deny my soul path, I ended up suffering and taking people down with me.

Wolf Moondance, a shaman, read my astrological chart and said that those who are "called" to minister to other souls have to fulfill their duty or else they manifest disease or tragedy in their lives. Sort of like an unconscious death wish. She said, "You cannot NOT love, Vicky."

This is... the trajectory of power. Compassion.

When harnessed, it becomes a beacon and a fountain of everlasting life. Joy.

We have no choice as humans. We must BE love. For me, this means being STOKED and using my life to help people have FUN, even in the midst of their pain which I call "holiness" and this intense learning curve called life.

Mahalo Nui
Deepest Thanks

<u>To those who are living:</u>

Wolf Moondance, author
Samantha Khury, animal communicator
Stanley Ibrao, energetic medicine healer
Ben Latuperissa, retired top secret agent
Gregory James, author of "The Way Home"
Errin Gilliland, beauty scientist
Grace Walker, Honokaa Trading Company on Big Island, Hawaii
Cidel Alexander Lord, tita
Keahi Kanakahi, fisherman
Bunny Kahanamoku, prophet
Sue Chau, college roommate
Richard Firmey, organic farmer
Bernie, apple grower
Dahli and Henry Taylor, street people and wise friends
Wendell, homeless compost man
Taro Patch Ohana (Watari and Tai Hook family, Mike Woods, Shorty)
Uncle Calvin Saffrey, himself
Dana Kauai'iki Olores, hula kumu
Chilla Chad Wiegle, lei maker

<u>To those who have passed:</u>

Jimmy Kuen Chen Lee, my father
Lewellyn Nohili Yadao, friend and hanai uncle
Jason Tai Young Kamapua'a Lee, my son

<u>To those who are forever:</u>

God of humanity, Father & Mother God
Pelehonuamea, volcano goddess
Dr. Hansen and the Casa da Fraternidade de Sao Francisco de Assis
Namolokama, mountain
Black Elk, Lakota guardian
Stradavarius and my entire dream team of spirit guides
Ke Kalo o ke Hanalei, the taro
Kaua'i, beloved island

HTTP://WEB.ME.COM/VISIONBOARD

ABOUT THE AUTHOR

Olivia Vicky Lee (1974 to present)

Olivia Vicky Lee graduated from U.C. Berkeley with honors when she was 20 years old, where she majored in Rhetoric and minored in Asian American Studies. She intended to enroll at Harvard Divinity for a master's degree and was guaranteed acceptance and financial aide, by a group of religious studies professors and graduate students from various Ivy League schools who monitored her work. Her proposed area of study was Feminine Liberation Theology. When her father died of cancer in 1997, she walked away from her studies.

She then trained in an advanced clairvoyant program at Aesclepion Meditation Center in San Rafael, C.A., for 5 years to learn how to control her psychic ability. When she was 24, she opened an organic juice bar in Berkeley, CA called Raw Energy. It was 60 square feet and grossed $120,000 per year. It became a hub of the community where customers would buy a $4 fresh-squeezed juice and receive one free psychic reading.

Four years later, she sold her business to move to Hawai'i where she became a taro farmer with a family of native Hawaiians. She also travelled to Brazil and lived in a monastery there, for a year.

Taro Patch Small Press
Coming Soon!

Workbook #1 Supplement: cracking the money/doubt code   **Workbook #2: Respect vs. Love**

New Vision Board Workbooks